Letts EXPLORE

A Letts Literature Guide

Every effort has been made to trace copyright holders and to obtain their permisssion for the use of copyright material. The author and publishers will gladly receive information enabling them to rectify any reference or credit in subsequent editions.

First published 1994
Reprinted 1994, 1996, 2002

Letts Educational
414 Chiswick High Road
London W4 5TF
Telephone: 020 8996 3333

Typeset by Jordan Publishing Design

Self-test questions devised by Claire Wright

Text design Jonathan Barnard

Cover and text illustrations Hugh Marshall

Graphic illustration Ian Foulis and Associates, Barbara Linton

ISBN 1 85758 249 7

British Library Cataloguing in Publication Data
A CIP record for this book is available from the British Library.

Printed and bound in Great Britain by
Ashford Colour Press Ltd, Gosport, Hants

Letts Educational Limited is a division of Granada Learning Limited, part of the Granada Media Group.

Contents

Plot synopsis

The play is set in ancient Rome, in Italy. Rome's leader, Julius Caesar, has come back from a successful series of campaigns against Pompey. It seems likely that Caesar may be made king.

Some of Rome's aristocratic noblemen (patricians) are worried that Caesar is too ambitious and they plot against him. Cassius leads the conspiracy, joined by Cinna, Casca and some others. They hope to get the highly respected Marcus Brutus to join them in killing Caesar on the Ides (15th) of March in the Capitol building where they fear that Rome's senators will name Caesar as king. Caesar's wife Calphurnia and Brutus' wife Portia (who don't know anything about the plot) both have premonitions that something bad is going to happen. Calphurnia tries to persuade Caesar to stay home that day, saying she has had fearful dreams. One of the plotters – Decius Brutus – reassures Caesar that he shouldn't worry about his wife's dreams and persuades Caesar to go to the Capitol buildings. In the Capitol the plotters distract Caesar's close and trusted friend Mark Antony while they stab Caesar to death. They smear Caesar's blood on their hands and weapons and walk among the people, saying that peace and freedom are now safe.

Antony secretly vows revenge and persuades Brutus to let him make a speech at Caesar's funeral. At the funeral Brutus makes a speech first, to persuade the people that Caesar had to be killed to save Rome from his ambitions to become a tyrant king. Brutus then leaves Antony alone with the crowd and Antony persuades them that Caesar's murder was evil. The crowd turns on the plotters, who are forced to escape with their followers from Rome.

Antony forms a triumvirate (rule by three people) with Octavius, Caesar's nephew, and they draw up a list of the traitors who must die and set off with an army to catch them. In the plotters' camp Brutus and Cassius fall out over how to fight the coming battle. Brutus learns that his wife Portia has taken her own life. Caesar's ghost appears to Brutus and says it will see him again at Philippi. The armies meet at Philippi and at first Brutus' side seems to be winning. But Cassius thinks that Brutus has been defeated and, fearing he is surrounded, has his servant kill him. Brutus is finally defeated but takes his own life before he can be captured, leaving Antony victorious.

Characters and themes in *Julius Caesar*

Julius Caesar

The most powerful man in Rome at the start of the play. He is killed by a group of patricians who are afraid that his power threatens the republic.

Marcus Brutus

A republican patrician (aristocrat) who joins the conspiracy for high-minded and public-spirited reasons. Brutus is concerned always to behave honourably but is politically naive.

Caius Cassius

One of Caesar's assassins. A shrewd, quick-thinking, practical politician, who, nevertheless, defers fatally to Brutus. Bitterly envious of Caesar, he is the main architect of the conspiracy.

Mark Antony

Caesar's loyal lieutenant. A shrewd and calculating man who pursues the assassins mercilessly to their deaths. A confident general who is very skilled at manipulating others.

Octavius Caesar

Julius Caesar's nephew and legal heir. He joins forces with Mark Antony to defeat the conspirators. He will, at the end of the play, become Caesar Augustus, the first and greatest of the Roman emperors.

Portia

Portia

The wife of Brutus. A devoted woman who eventually commits suicide because she is afraid for her husband.

Friendship

Friendship

Fate and the supernatural

Fate and the supernatural

Order, disorder and power

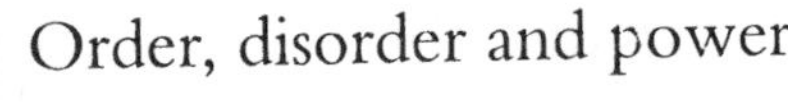

Order, disorder and power

Act One
MARCH XV
CONSPIRATORS
TREBONIVS
DECIVS BRVTVS
CINNA
METELLVS CIMBER
CASSIVS
BRVTVS
Act 1 Scene 1
The soothsayer warns Caesar: 'Beware the Ides of March!'
Caesar is outwardly pleased to refuse the crown. But inside he feels…what?
Casca describes the terrible visions seen during the storm:
CONSPIRATORS
TREBONIVS
DECIVS BRVTVS
CINNA
METELLVS CIMBER
CASSIVS
BRVTVS
CASCA
Act 1 Scene 3 –
…a slave with a flaming hand which did not burn, a lion which did not attack, men all covered in fire…
Act Two
The conspirators plot the murder of Caesar as a fiery dawn breaks
JULIUS CAESAR DIED MARCH 15TH
CASCA
ASSASSINATION AGREED
15TH MARCH
Calphurnia dreams of Caesar's murder. Dawn breaks on the Ides of March
Act Three
FRIENDS, ROMANS, COUNTRYMEN,
'…my statue,
Which, like a fountain w
an hundred spouts,
Did run pure blood; and
many lusty Romans
Came smiling, and did ba
their hands in it.'
YOU TOO BRUTUS?
Cowards die many times before their deaths; The valiant never taste of death but once.

MARCH
XV
Well, soothsayer – the Ides of March are come!
Aye, Caesar – but not yet gone…
t 3 Scene 1
e killing of an
ogant, unfeeling, callous
nt – or the cowardly murder
strong and courageous ruler?
'Peace, freedom, and liberty!'
Act 3 Scene 2
'Let slip the dogs of war'
Act Four
REVENGE
Caesar's spirit is released – hot from hell and ranging for revenge
TRAITORS WHO MVST DIE
BRVTVS CASSIVS PVBLIVS
The crazed mob flee to seek the conspirators
WAR
PHILIPPI 14 KM
Act Five
Act 5 Scene 2
Cassius and Brutus face Antony and Octavius. Insults are exchanged, then…
PHILIPPI
Omens of bad luck greet the army of Cassius and Brutus
…the two armies clash in battle!
BRVTVS CASSIVS
The conspirators fall…
'O Julius Caesar, thou art mighty yet!'

Who's who in *Julius Caesar*

Julius Caesar

At the start of the play Caesar has returned victorious from battle in the civil war against Pompey and is Rome's supreme military leader. Yet, as the play progresses, a different picture appears of a man who is deaf in one ear, who suffers from epilepsy and who in private is superstitious.

Caesar maintains a public image of being a god-like creature, and this attitude causes resentment amongst some of the aristocratic republicans. One side of Caesar is arrogant and easily flattered. He does not foresee the assassination because he does not understand the feelings of those around him. In this sense he is a poor politician. The other side of Caesar cares for the common people and attaches great importance to loyalty. He is a good reader of character, as is shown by his summing up of Cassius in the second scene of Act 1. In this sense, he is an adept politician who plays to the crowd with great success. After the assassination he appears as a ghost to Brutus and his spirit dominates the subsequent action.

Marcus Brutus

The key to Brutus' character is his huge moral authority in the eyes of others. To Romans he embodies all the old republican virtues, especially that of disinterested public service. This explains why Cassius and the others are anxious to involve him in the plot; why Cassius is happy for him to be the public leader of the conspiracy; why, when he wishes to kill himself at the end of the play, he finds it difficult to get anyone to help him; and why even Antony is moved to speak a tribute to him over his corpse. Brutus is a rather idealistic dreamer who is proud of his own disciplined thinking. By appealing to people's reason he assumes he can persuade them to the right course of action. He underrates the importance of emotion in other people's behaviour and assumes that they can suppress their feelings as well as he can. He dreams that one day Rome will return to the way it was in some golden age in the past.

He has no personal ambition and the world of intrigue and power-politics is alien to him. He is politically naive and lacks ruthlessness. Once in a position of power, he makes mistake after mistake and shows his inexperience, although he continues to act from what he thinks are the best motives. In a fatal error of judgement, he insists that Antony be allowed to live, although the more astute Cassius advises against it. He thinks that corruption has been driven out after the assassination and is outraged by the way Cassius thinks they should turn a blind eye to it.

Caius Cassius

Cassius is an aristocratic member of Roman society with an aritocrat's contempt for the common people. Deeply envious of Caesar, his plot against him is driven by self-interest, in contrast to the motives that drive Brutus. Cassius manipulates other people and is happy to allow others to think that they are really in control. Cassius sees people as they really are and uses their weaknesses to gain influence over them. (See the way he manipulates Brutus in Act 2 Sc 2 and Casca in Act 1 Sc 3.)

Cassius' view of himself and the way he uses others are revealed in his soliloquy at the end of Act 1 Sc 2. But he miscalculates his ability to control Brutus. He realises too late that the omens were always against him and under pressure he gives way to panic and takes his own life.

Mark Antony

The first impression you are given of Mark Antony is of an idle playboy and a crony of Caesar. This is clearly an underestimation because, after the assassination of Caesar, Antony emerges as a skilful speaker and a clever general. Brutus makes a fatal error in not having Antony put to death after the assassination, believing him to be harmless. As a result of Antony's 'Friends, Romans, countrymen...' speech the conspirators flee from Rome and he raises an army to pursue them. He becomes Caesar's avenging angel and joins forces with Octavius to form an army that eventually defeats Brutus and Cassius. At the end Antony acknowledges the unselfishness of Brutus' motives and speaks a moving tribute over his corpse.

Octavius Caesar

Octavius is the nephew of Julius Caesar and his heir. He arrives in Rome too late to stop the assassination of Caesar, but joins forces with Mark Antony to pursue and kill the conspirators. He, Antony and Lepidius form the triumvirate that rules Rome after the assassination. Octavius shows himself to be a strong character; he refuses to allow Antony to give him orders on the field of battle and decides for himself which side of the battlefield he will fight on. He speaks the final lines of the play, emphasising that, with his victory, order, dignity and honourable rule have returned.

Portia

Portia is the wife of Brutus. She is the daughter of Cato, a famous fighter for Rome who killed himself rather than be captured. She sees herself as inheriting her father's best qualities. She is determined to share her husband's worries, demands that he treat her as a proper partner in their marriage and wounds herself in the thigh to show how she is able to bear pain. Although a strong and determined woman, she worries about Brutus. She becomes almost hysterical as the time of the assassination draws near. True to her character even in death, Portia commits suicide in a way requiring great courage – she swallows burning coals.

Calphurnia

Calphurnia is the wife of Julius Caesar. She is a weaker character than Portia. Calphurnia worries about her husband all the time and is plagued by frightening dreams. She has a premonition that Caesar is to be assassinated and almost succeeds in persuading him not to go to the senate on the day that the assassins plan to kill him.

Casca

One of the chief conspirators. Brutus is told by Cassius that Casca's blunt manner is deceiving and that he is really a reliable general. Casca is witty and sarcastic about what he sees as Caesar's overblown opinion of himself. He is superstitious, easily frightened by all the bad omens he has seen and heard about. He is easily manipulated by Cassius, who persuades him into becoming involved in the conspiracy.

Cicero

Cicero is calm, clear-thinking and well respected by people who see him as an elder statesman. During the storm, he meets the terrified Casca and speaks one of the most telling lines in the play: 'men may construe things after their fashion, clean from the purpose of the things themselves' (3, 1). Cicero knows that people often see only what they want – this turns out to be true of a great many characters in the play.

Cinna

There are two characters called Cinna in the play. The first is one of the conspirators who is used to carry forged messages to Brutus from Cassius. The second is a harmless poet who, following Antony's speech in the forum, is stopped by the mob and killed, simply for having the same name as the well-known conspirator.

Decius Brutus

Decius Brutus is the messenger who comes to fetch Caesar, thus ensuring that he attends the senate on the day the murderers plan to kill him. He is skilful with words and persuades Caesar that the dreams of Calphurnia, far from predicting danger, are in fact good omens.

Flavius and Marullus

These are the two tribunes you meet at the start of the play. Tribunes were elected by the common people to look after their interests, but Flavius and Marullus rebuke the workmen for taking a holiday to celebrate the return of Caesar to Rome. They remove some of the decorations hung on Caesar's statues and for this Caesar puts them to death.

Lepidus

Lepidus is a rich general who, with Antony and Octavius, forms the triumvirate which rules Rome after the assassination of Caesar. Although he is involved in making the death-list of people to be executed after Caesar's murder, Antony thinks little of him.

Ligarius

Ligarius arrives late at Brutus' house near the start of the play. He has been very ill but seems magically cured when

Brutus asks him to join the conspiracy. He blindly accepts the leadership of Brutus and is an example of the power that Brutus' good reputation has over others.

Lucilius

Lucilius is one of Brutus' officers and to prevent Brutus being captured, he pretends to be Brutus. Antony recognises that he is not Brutus but is impressed with Lucilius' loyalty.

Lucius

Lucius is the young boy who is Brutus' servant. He emphasises the calm and gentle side of Brutus' character as he sings and plays music for him. He appears at times of stress for Brutus, reminding him of the innocent life he has given up because of the conspiracy.

Pindarus

Cassius captured Pindarus in a battle at Parthia and made him his servant. At the end of the play Cassius gives Pindarus his freedom in return for his help in committing suicide.

Popilius Lena

Popilius is the senator who panics Cassius by telling him that he wishes Cassius' 'enterprise' good luck. When he talks to Caesar, Cassius is terrified that he is telling him about the plot. In fact Popilius is simply chatting to Caesar.

Strato

Having tried several other servants and friends, Brutus finally turns to the loyal Strato and succeeds in persuading him to help him commit suicide.

Titinius

Titinius is one of Cassius's officers whom Cassius sends to discover whether some approaching soldiers are friends or enemies. Before he can return Cassius despairs and takes his own life. Returning, Titinius also commits suicide.

Volumnius

Brutus and Volumnius have known each other since they were both at school together. He refuses to help Brutus commit suicide because he does not think it is a proper thing for an old friend to do.

Themes and images in *Julius Caesar*

Themes are the important ideas that run through the play. You will come across them many times. They connect together the story, the characters and the different scenes in the play.

When words and descriptions suggest a picture in your mind, that is called an **image**. Images are often used to make an idea stronger, or to encourage you to think of things from a particular point of view. If you described someone as being 'as skinny as a stick' or as behaving 'like a wild animal' you would be using simple images.

Shakespeare was a great writer who used themes and images a lot. Many of the examples you will find are very striking and impressive. Other examples will be less obvious, so you will need to pay careful attention to the language that Shakespeare has used. Read the following notes carefully.

Friendship

Friendship

Several characters realise – usually too late – that, like Caesar, they have either placed too much trust in friendship, or have not realised how important it is in their lives, like Cassius and Brutus. One of the main themes in the play is about how the world falls in ruins around people when friendship and loyalty are replaced by disloyalty and mistrust. Part of the play argues that people should value friendship more than their principles and that they should forgive people their weaknesses rather than put unrealistic expectation upon them. As Caesar, then Cassius, then Brutus each face death one by one, they talk about the importance of loyalty and friendship.

Fate and the supernatural

Fate and the supernatural

The play is full of examples of prophecies and warnings which characters ignore at their peril. The play argues that the lives of people are controlled by powers that they cannot understand and cannot control. These powers – or fate – give them clear warnings when they are straying from correct behaviour, either through dreams and visions, like those of Calphurnia, or through priests and soothsayers who can sometimes predict danger. Sometimes the warnings come through terrible storms or other signs from above that all is not well, as Casca sees during the storm in Act 1 Sc 3. Not every character in the play believes in omens or fate at first, but eventually they all do, especially Cassius who realises his mistake too late at the end of his life, when he dies on his birthday.

Order, disorder and power

Order, disorder and power

People in Shakespeare's time thought that every person or thing in the world had a proper place or position which was decided by God. The conspirators' main crime is that they upset this natural order by murdering Caesar and the powers of heaven then punish them. Order and peace should be the natural state of the world, according to this view, and therefore after Caesar's murder chaos and confusion run wild on earth.

The play contains many examples of order and disorder and the struggle for power – the play opens with talk about the aftermath of the rebellion and civil war. Depending on your point of view, you can see some characters as forces either for order or for disorder. Caesar is seen by some characters as a force for disorder, a self-seeking tyrant who wants to be set up as a king with total power and whom they are lucky to have killed in time to stop him. Others see Caesar as the people's hero who was murdered by traitors or rebels who were only seeking power for themselves. Antony and Brutus can be seen as two different people who are both seeking in their different ways to overthrow what they see as tyranny. Each of them sees himself as the saviour of the common people and therefore as a force for good. Much of the action of the play revolves around arguments about liberty versus tyranny, or the old order versus the new order, or about the use and abuse of power. Often the issues are to do with what is best for an individual's private benefit and what is best for the benefit of the people as a whole. Usually it is the case that both causes cannot be served at the same time.

Text commentary

Act 1 Scene 1

Julius Caesar is having a triumphant procession through Rome to celebrate his victory in the civil war.

Disloyalty

Order, disorder and power

The play starts just after the end of a terrible civil war, when the republic of Rome tore itself apart. The ordinary working people of Rome have decided to take a holiday to celebrate Caesar's return to Rome. They are confronted by two Tribunes, Flavius and Marullus. The cobbler outwits Flavius by teasing him with his clever puns. This amusing section gives a flavour of more serious things to come, when other figures in authority are not respected but are violently overthrown instead.

Flavius and Marullus say that the people should be busy working, not wandering about in their best clothes enjoying themselves. They are angry because it is not long since the people used to celebrate the return of Pompey after he had won great victories. Now they want to celebrate the return of Caesar, who has just conquered the sons of Pompey. Flavius and Marullus say this is disloyal. Romans should not celebrate the victory of one Roman over another.

The ordinary working people

Marullus says the people are like 'blocks' or 'stones' and are 'worse than senseless things'. He reminds them how they used to cheer when Pompey returned from battle. He tells the people that they are not thinking, and tells them to go home and pray that a plague is not sent to punish them for their ingratitude.

About the Feast of Lupercal

Order, disorder and power

The common people would have decorated the streets and statues of Rome ready for the feast of Lupercal. This celebration was held every year on 15th February in honour of Lupercus, the god of fertility and flocks. Marullus and Flavius decide to remove from the statues of Caesar the flowers and decorations put there by the people. They do not want it to look as though Caesar's return is being celebrated.

Is Caesar too ambitious?

Marullus and Flavius accuse Caesar of wanting to become all-powerful, to 'soar above the view of men' and 'keep us all in servile fearfulness'. Some important people in Rome are clearly worried about this possibility. This introduces the controversial question of the extent of Caesar's power, one of the main forces in the action of the play.

Order, disorder and power

An example of the power of words

Notice how quickly the common people are influenced by what they are told. They are easily manipulated. One minute they are happily seeking a day off from work and the next they are creeping off home after being scolded by Marullus. This is the first of several occasions in the play when the common people are swayed by the power of words.

Act 1 Scene 2

Caesar goes to the Forum to see the celebrations for the feast of Lupercal. On the way a fortune-teller warns Caesar to beware March 15th (the Ides of March). We are told that Caesar refuses to be crowned king at the celebrations and becomes ill. Cassius starts his efforts to persuade Brutus to join with those who are against Caesar.

Caesar is superstitious

Part of the celebrations during the feast of Lupercal was a race. Caesar tells his wife Calphurnia to stand where the runners will pass. Antony is one of the runners and Caesar asks him to remember to touch Calphurnia as he passes her because, according to legend, this will cure her of the curse of sterility.

Caesar does not heed warnings

Fate and the supernatural

On the way to the race Caesar meets a soothsayer, a kind of fortune-teller who was thought to be able to see into the future. The soothsayer tells Caesar to be careful on the 15th of March (known as the Ides of March), but Caesar dismisses him.

Notice that here it is Brutus who gives Caesar the soothsayer's warning. This is one of the play's many examples of dramatic irony; it is Brutus who later becomes one of Caesar's murderers.

Later on Caesar tells Antony privately that he is deaf in his left ear. Caesar is partly deaf in more ways than one; a criticism of him as a leader could be that he hears only what he wants to hear. Notice how everyone must obey Caesar's every command.

Caesar in public and Caesar in private

Caesar's public behaviour differs from his private behaviour. It could be that he feels that in public he is expected to behave the way he does. Publicly he ignores the soothsayer as a 'dreamer', privately he hopes that his wife will be cured of infertility as part of the ritual surrounding the race during the feast of Lupercal.

Cassius and Brutus

Brutus and Cassius stay behind as Caesar and his party go on to the race. Cassius says that Brutus has not seemed himself lately. Brutus apologises, saying that he has been preoccupied. Notice how careful Cassius is in the way he approaches Brutus on the subject of Caesar.

How well does Brutus know himself?

Cassius first asks Brutus if he can see his own face. When Brutus says that people can only see themselves reflected in other things, Cassius has got the answer he wanted. He tells Brutus that everyone has great respect for him. Their conversation is interrupted by the shouts of the crowd and Brutus says he 'fears' Caesar has been chosen as King of Rome. Cassius sees another chance and wonders whether Brutus would disapprove of this. Brutus says he would, even though Caesar is someone he 'loves well'.

Brutus says he loves honour more than life

Brutus asks Cassius what it was he wanted to talk to him about, saying that if is to do with the good of the people, he will listen because that is an honourable cause and Brutus loves honour more than life. Cassius says it *is* about honour but, as he goes on, it becomes clear that he is, in fact, talking about his own honour (self-respect), sense of injustice and jealousy of Caesar's growing power.

Cassius resents Caesar

Order, disorder and power

Cassius says that he could not bear to be alive if he were the sort of person who was in awe of another man. He talks about how he, Caesar and Brutus were all born free, eat the same food and feel the cold as much as each other. He describes how he once saved Caesar from the river when they were trying to swim across it. On another occasion whilst in Spain, Cassius says Caesar fell ill from fever and cried out like 'a sick girl'. Cassius is pointing out that this ordinary man Caesar is now treated as a god, whilst Cassius is just a 'wretched creature'. Although he starts by appealing to Brutus' sense of right and wrong, he ends by talking about his own envy.

Fate and the supernatural

Cassius compares Caesar to a 'colossus' and says ordinary men have become like small creatures 'peeping about' for 'dishonourable graves' for themselves. He is careful not to appeal to Brutus' personal ambition because he knows that Brutus has none. He says that ordinary Romans have become 'underlings' not because it is their fate, but because they have allowed this situation to arise.

Is Brutus innocent or is he cunning?

Brutus indicates he has had similar thoughts himself but is non-committal about what course of action he will take. Brutus is at pains to tell Cassius how 'honourable' he is but then suggests he is half-persuaded by Cassius' arguments. He says he'd rather be a poor villager than live in a Rome under a dictatorship. Does Brutus really understand what Cassius is driving at (that Caesar should be overthrown), or is he just playing for time?

Cassius has a 'lean and hungry' look

Order, disorder and power

Caesar and his party come back from the games. Caesar looks angry, Calphurnia is pale, Cicero seems furious and everyone else looks very subdued. Caesar remarks to Antony that Cassius looks lean and hungry; he prefers men around him who are fat. He thinks Cassius is dangerous. Antony reassures him, saying that Cassius is not to be feared and that he is a noble Roman. But Caesar would seem to be a good judge of character, given the conversation that has just taken place.

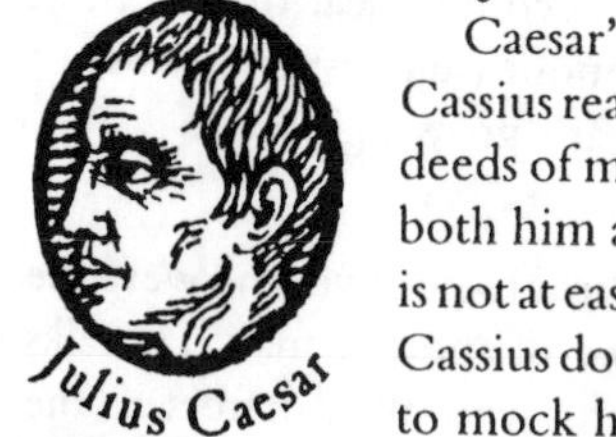

Caesar's summary of Cassius is interesting: he says that Cassius reads a lot, is observant and 'looks quite through the deeds of men'. If Caesar is correct, then Cassius has judged both him and Brutus shrewdly. Caesar judges that Cassius is not at ease with himself, and he attributes it to the fact that Cassius does not like plays or music and never smiles except to mock himself.

Although Caesar claims that he isn't frightened of Cassius, notice that he emphasises how such men should be feared. It could be that Caesar really is privately afraid of Cassius but refuses to admit it in public.

Caesar refuses the crown

Brutus detains Casca and asks him what went on during the race to make everyone look so agitated. Casca says that Caesar was offered a crown three times but each time refused it. Although it was not a real crown, because Rome did not have a king, and seemed to be offered in jest, it appeared that Caesar was being asked symbolically to become King of Rome. The crowd were pleased that he refused the crown, although Casca says he thinks Caesar really wanted to accept it. It may be that Caesar was angry that he had to refuse publicly to be King of Rome.

Caesar has a fit

Casca found the episode amusing and tells how Caesar then fell down and had a fit in the marketplace. Casca puts Caesar's sudden illness down to the fact that the common people are a sweaty rabble who have such 'stinking breath' that Caesar could not breathe.

Julius Caesar

Casca says that when Caesar recovered he apologised for his behaviour and for anything he might have said to upset anyone. The crowd were so sympathetic towards him that they would have forgiven him anything.

Ordinary people

Order, disorder and power

Casca, like most of those who plot against Caesar, seems more interested in preserving his own position and privileges than in looking after the rights of the ordinary working people. Casca is very harsh towards the common people but, to be fair to him, you should note that later on in Act 3 Scs 1 and 2 the common people do behave in a very fickle and brutal way.

Cicero is careful

Casca says that because Cicero spoke in Greek, he cannot tell what he said about Caesar's behaviour. It seems that Cicero spoke Greek so that only his close friends would understand and Casca says they all smiled at what was being said. Cassius arranges to talk again to Casca the following day.

More about the clever use of words

Brutus finds Casca a 'blunt fellow' but Cassius says Casca is deliberately forthright so that people will pay more attention to what he says; he denies that Casca is either coarse or stupid. This is another example of words being used to sway others. It is the same skill that Cassius has just been using on Brutus. Cassius understands Casca's trick well; he is, as Caesar noted, 'a great observer' who sees clearly 'through the deeds of men'.

What kind of man is Cassius?

Cassius speaks the play's first soliloquy. He is satisfied that he will be able to win Brutus over to the conspiracy against Caesar. He decides to arrange for

messages to be thrown through Brutus' window that night. The writing will be disguised so they will appear to be from various citizens, praising Brutus and hinting that Caesar is becoming too ambitious. It is not easy to tell whether Cassius is pleased because he thinks he has successfully corrupted Brutus or whether he is sad that such a noble person can be 'seduced' away from what he knows is right.

What kind of man is Brutus?

If you feel Brutus is honourable and innocent, you will see him as a tragic figure who is toppled from his high position in society by an evil he does not really understand. But if you think Brutus knows exactly what he is getting into, you may see him as a clever politician who pretends to be innocent whilst actually being corrupt. Try to decide what in the play so far has made you feel the way you do.

You meet **Caesar** for the first time and get contradictory impressions of him. He is a superstitious man who believes that his wife is not bearing him children because she is suffering from a curse of infertility. He seems a proud man who boasts he is not afraid of other people because he is who he is. He frequently talks about himself in what is called the 'third person', as when he turns to the soothsayer and instead of saying 'Go on, I am listening', says, 'Speak. Caesar is turned to hear'. This makes him appear arrogant. This great 'colossus', as Cassius calls him, is also deaf in his left ear and prone to fall down and foam at the mouth. Somebody has had Marullus and Flavius 'put to silence' (killed) for taking the decorations off Caesar's statues. You are not told who this somebody was but you might suspect that it was Caesar, or that he approved of it. This hints at the efficient but brutal way Caesar retains his grip on power. Other evidence shows Caesar in a better light. He refuses the Kingship of Rome three times. Perhaps he is not so ambitious after all. Casca says he thought Caesar wanted to accept the crown really, but you will have to make your own mind up, once you have decided how reliable Casca is.

Act 1 Scene 3

A terrible storm rages. Cassius tells Casca it is a sign of the gods' displeasure with Caesar.

The storm

Order, disorder and power

It is evening and a terrifying storm is raging. Cicero meets Casca, who describes the amazing sights he has seen – fire falling from the sky, a slave whose hand seemed on fire but did not burn, and a lion that walked by and did not attack him. He met some frightened women who told him they had seen men all covered in fire walking up and down the streets. These and the owl that hooted and shrieked at noon the previous day in the marketplace are all omens to Casca.

The meaning of the storm

Fate and the supernatural

You might like to think about what these events would have represented to Shakespeare's audience. The Elizabethans thought that occurrences in the heavens were omens of things happening on earth. The storm could symbolise the upheaval that is about to occur when Caesar is murdered and the state is thrown into chaos. The lion could be Caesar, prowling the streets of Rome, and the burning men could be images showing the fate of the conspirators, condemned to walk about in the fires of hell for their crimes. Evil seems to have been set loose by the wicked thoughts of a few individuals, or possibly because Caesar seeks to become king.

Cicero brushes off Casca's worries by saying that people tend to read into such matters what they want to, irrespective of what the events really mean. Perhaps Casca's guilty conscience is making him afraid. Casca says that Caesar is going to the Capitol tomorrow. Cicero leaves and Cassius enters.

Cassius says the storm is a warning

Cassius says he is not frightened by the storm. In fact he has walked about in it, baring his chest in the path of the lightning. Casca is amazed and asks him why he has tempted the anger of the gods in such a frightening way. Cassius says Casca is afraid of the storm only because he does not understand the true cause of it. He says that the world is filled with such strange events, which are a warning to mankind.

Order, disorder and power

Cassius says the storm and other fearful events show the disapproval of the gods. The heavens are torn apart by the storm because the Roman empire is being torn apart. Cassius says these omens actually describe what is wrong on earth. He says he can think of a man who would fit such a description.

Notice that Cassius – who, according to Caesar 'hears no music' – is at home in the middle of the violence of the storm. Cassius is not associated with 'civilised' things like music, poetry or gentle laughter, but with dangerous and unnatural events: disorder, death and destruction.

Caesar must not be crowned king

As Cassius complains that the Roman people have become weak, Casca says that he has heard that the senators intend to make Caesar king the next day. This only infuriates Cassius further and he says that if this happens he will kill himself. Without realising the irony of what he is saying, he describes not only how the gods will strengthen his own determination, but also how they will increase the power of the people to overthrow tyrants: 'Therein, ye gods, you make the weak most strong;/Therein, ye gods, you tyrants do defeat.'

'To make a mighty fire, begin with weak straws'

Order, disorder and power

Cassius says that the current terrible state of affairs is not actually Caesar's fault. It is the fault of the people, who have become weak. Caesar behaves like a wolf only because the people behave like sheep; he is like a lion only when surrounded by hinds (meaning deer, but also meaning low-born people or servants). Cassius is very scathing of Rome, calling it rubbish and offal. He says it is only because Rome has fallen to such depths that 'so vile a thing as Caesar' has become powerful and admired by the people.

Casca swears to join with Cassius in his cause and stay with him to the end. Cassius tells him that several of the 'noblest-minded' citizens are with them and are waiting at Pompey's Porch. For the first time Cassius openly admits that what they are planning to do is 'most bloody, fiery, and most terrible.' Cinna, another of the conspirators, enters. Cassius sends him to take papers and messages to where Brutus will find them and arranges to meet him later at Pompey's Porch.

Everything hangs on Brutus joining the conspiracy

Cassius tells Casca how certain he is that Brutus will join their conspiracy. Casca agrees that he will be a valuable addition to their cause. If Brutus were seen to be involved in overthrowing Caesar, the people would accept it as a noble and honourable deed. Casca knows that without the involvement of Brutus the people would see the violent overthrow of Caesar as a crime. Cassius is being rather reckless and over-confident here because Brutus has not yet committed himself to join the conspiracy.

> **Cassius** is the chief organiser of the plot against Caesar and that night, during a terrible storm, he recruits Casca to the conspiracy. **The storm** terrifies Casca and many other Romans, but not Cassius or Cicero. The storm is, according to Cassius, both a message from the gods and a symbol of what is wrong on earth. He does not see that it could equally be a warning to the conspirators. Cassius is unafraid of the risks he is taking. He says that as the people of Rome have become too slavish to help themselves, he will have to act for them. He seems passionate in his belief that what he is doing is right. Cassius tells Casca that he is certain that Brutus will be persuaded to join, but this is a little over-optimistic. Everything depends on Brutus being part of the plot. Notice the irony of where the conspirators choose to meet to plot against Caesar – *Pompey's* Porch.

Self-test (Questions) Act One

Uncover the plot

Delete two of the three alternatives given, to find the correct plot. Beware possible misconceptions and muddles.

Caesar/Antony/Octavius is coming back to Rome in triumph after defeating Publius/Messala/Pompey in the civil wars. With his followers, he goes to the Senate/Forum/Capitol to see the celebrations of the feast of Lucretia/Livorno/Lupercal, and on the way a soothsayer tells him to beware the Nones of March/Calends of May/Ides of March. Caesar refuses the crown/robe of honour/laurel wreath at the celebrations. Cinna/Clitus/Cassius tries to persuade Brutus to join with those who are against Caesar by saying that Caesar is ambitious/evil/unpopular. Cassius and Casca arrange to meet later at the Arch of Titus/Pompey's Porch/Brutus' house.

Why? Who? Where? What? How?

1 Why is Flavius angry with the common people?
2 Who has Caesar just conquered?
3 Where must Calpurnia stand, and why?
4 What two examples of Caesar's human weakness does Cassius give?
5 Why is Caesar suspicious of Cassius? (Give seven reasons)
6 How many times does Casca say that Caesar refused the crown?
7 Who offered Caesar the crown?
8 What five unnatural sights have been seen before and during the storm?
9 How does Cassius interpret the storm?
10 What does Cassius say he will do if Caesar becomes king?

Who said that?

1 Who said: 'You blocks, you stones, you worse than senseless things!'?
2 Who said: 'He is a dreamer; let us leave him: pass'?
3 Who said: 'Brutus will start a spirit as soon as Caesar'?
4 Who said: 'Come on my right hand, for this ear is deaf'?
5 Who said: 'It is the part of men to fear and tremble'?

Open quotes

Find the line – and complete the phrase or sentence.

1 'When Caesar says, "do this,"...'
2 'poor Brutus, with himself at war...'
3 'I had as lief not be...'
4 'The fault, dear Brutus...'
5 'Nor airless dungeon, nor strong links of iron...'

Prove it!

Find a quote from the text that could be used to back up each of the following statements.

1 Brutus shares Cassius' anxiety about the current state of Rome.
2 Caesar is not superstitious.
3 Brutus is held in high regard by the people of Rome

On the other hand...

Find a quote from the text that could be used to argue against each of the following statements.

1 Caesar is ambitious.
2 Cassius has Rome's best interests at heart.
3 The people of Rome remain loyal to their leader.

A sense of history

1 Which two characters refer to Pompey in this Act?
2 Who refers to Aeneas, and in what context?
3 Things are not as they were in Rome – find two quotes which tell you this.

Interpreting the signs

Find EIGHT instances of characters reading the signs during this Act, whether from people's looks and behaviour, or from events in nature.

Self-test (Answers) Act One

Uncover the plot

Caesar is coming back to Rome in triumph, after defeating Pompey in the civil wars. With his followers, he goes to the Capitol to see the celebrations of the feast of Lupercal, and on the way a soothsayer tells him to beware the Ides of March. Caesar refuses the crown at the celebrations. Cassius tries to persuade Brutus to join with those who are against Caesar by saying that Caesar is ambitious. Cassius and Casca arrange to meet later at Pompey's Porch.

Why? Who? Where? What? How?

1 Because they have taken a holiday to celebrate Caesar's return to Rome
2 The sons of Pompey
3 Where Antony can touch her as he passes so that she may be cured of infertility
4 1 Cassius had to save Caesar from drowning because Caesar could not swim across the river Tiber
  2 Caesar nearly died from a fever when he was in Spain
5 1 He is thin; 2 he thinks too much; 3 he reads too much; 4 he 'looks quite through the deeds of men'; 5 he does not love plays; 6 he does not enjoy music; 7 he seldom smiles
6 Three times
7 Mark Antony
8 1 Fire has fallen from the sky; 2 a slave's hand was covered in flames but did not burn; 3 a lion walked past Casca but did not harm him; 4 a hundred women said they had seen men covered in flames; 5 an owl hooted and shrieked at noon in the marketplace
9 The heavens are angry because Caesar is becoming a tyrant
10 Cassius says he will take his own life

Who said that?

1 Marullus, a tribune 1,1
2 Caesar 1,2
3 Cassius 1,2
4 Caesar 1,2
5 Cassius 1,3

Open quotes

1 'When Caesar says, "do this," it is performed' 1,2
2 'poor Brutus, with himself at war,/Forgets the shows of love to other men.' 1,2
3 'I had as lief not be as live to be/In awe of such as thing as I myself.' 1,2
4 'The fault, dear Brutus, is not in our stars/ But in ourselves, that we are underlings.' 1,2
5 'Nor airless dungeon, nor strong links of iron/ Can be retentive to the strength of spirit' 1,3

Prove it!

1 'Brutus had rather be a villager/Than to repute himself a son of Rome/Under these hard conditions...' 1,2
2 'He is a dreamer; let us leave him: pass' 1,2
3 'O, he sits high in all the people's hearts' 1,3

On the other hand...

1 'Why, there was a crown offered him: and being offered him, he put it by with the back of his hand'
2 'Cassius from bondage will deliver Cassius'
3 'O you hard hearts, you cruel men of Rome,/ Knew you not Pompey?/'

A sense of history

1 Marullus 1,1; Cassius 1,2
2 Cassius compares his rescue of Caesar to Aeneas saving his father Anchises from Troy
3 1'Age, thou art shamed!/ Rome, thou hast lost the breed of noble bloods!' 1,2
  2'But, woe the while! our fathers' minds are dead,/ And we are govern'd with our mothers' spirits'1,3

Interpreting the signs

1 'He is a dreamer; let us leave him: pass' 1,2
2 'Brutus, I do observe you now of late:/I have not from your eyes that gentleness/And show of love as I was wont to have' 1,2
3 'I, your glass,/Will modestly discover to yourself/That of yourself which you yet know not of.'1,2
4 'The angry spot doth glow on Caesar's brow,/And all the rest look like a chidden train' 1,2
5 'men may construe things after their fashion,/Clean from the purpose of the things themselves' 1,3
6 'When the most mighty gods by tokens send/Such dreadful heralds to astonish us' 1,3
7 'the complexion of the element/In favour's like the work we have in hand' 1,3
8 'His countenance, like richest alchemy,/Will change to virtue and to worthiness.' 1,3

Act 2 Scene 1

Brutus decides that Caesar must be murdered. The conspirators arrive and detailed plans are agreed about who will and will not be killed: how, when and where.

Brutus cannot sleep

Like Caesar, Brutus is a man who in private has worries and doubts, but who in public is seen as strong and clear in his actions. Brutus has been awake all night thinking about what he should do about Caesar. He decides that Caesar must be killed; the solution to the problem 'must be by his death'. Notice the reasons Brutus gives for this. He says that Caesar's ruthlessness can only get worse with absolute power. He, Brutus, has no personal cause to 'spurn at' (kick against) Caesar, but that if Caesar becomes king he is sure to become a tyrant. Like 'the serpent's egg', he will become dangerous if allowed to grow.

When Brutus says 'it is the bright day that brings forth the adder' he intends the adder to be Caesar and the bright light to be Caesar as king. This is an example of dramatic irony, where the speaker's words have another meaning that they themselves do not understand; the poisonous adder is also Brutus or the other conspirators who will emerge into the bright day tomorrow.

Brutus' reasons

Because this is a soliloquy there is no other character on stage, so you should be clear that Brutus is attempting to persuade no one but himself here. How successful do you feel that he has been? Do you think his reasons are good enough for killing somebody? Notice how he first chooses a course of action and then thinks of reasons to justify it afterwards. Notice also how Brutus chooses words to make things seem less evil than they really are.

Although he has sent his servant Lucius to get a light for his chamber, Brutus never gets there because he is interrupted by the arrival of the conspirators in the darkness.

Lucius finds a letter to Brutus

Fate and the supernatural

Lucius returns with a paper he found thrown in at the window. It is one of the anonymous letters from Cassius. Lucius is sent to check whether the next day is the Ides of March. The letter urges Brutus to 'speak, strike, redress'. He remembers how his ancestors drove the last of the Tarquin kings from Rome and this makes him even more determined to strike against Caesar. Lucius returns and confirms that the next day is the Ides of March.

About the symbolism in the play

Brutus seems to blame Cassius for starting him off on his present train of

Order, disorder and power

thought. How true do you think this is? He says he has been unable to sleep since that time. Lucere means 'to light' in Latin and you should notice that the innocent Lucius has no difficulty sleeping. Brutus does not go towards his lighted room but remains in the darkness to greet the conspirators, underneath a sky filled with fire, in the 'hideous dream' he says he has been living in. The darkness, fire and Brutus' sleeplessness all have a symbolic significance. They represent the state of his mind and the darkness and the fiery sky are associated with the secrecy and evil of the conspiracy.

The conspirators: Brutus, Cassius, Trebonius, Decius Brutus, Casca, Cinna and Metellus Cimber

There is a knocking at the gate and Cassius and other conspirators enter. Several of the conspirators have 'their hats plucked about their ears' to hide their identity. Brutus comments that conspiracy is ashamed to show itself, even at night, 'when evils are most free'. Brutus is clearly unhappy at being involved with the conspirators but feels that circumstances make it necessary for the greater good. The conspirators are all carefully introduced and named by Cassius: Trebonius, Decius Brutus, Casca, Cinna and Metellus Cimber.

Dawn breaks on the Ides of March

Order, disorder and power

As Brutus and Cassius stand apart for a private discussion, the rest of the conspirators argue about where the sun is rising. The rising fire of the dawn marks the arrival of the day of Caesar's murder. Symbolically, Casca points to the rising sun with his sword.

Cassius says that they should all swear an oath of dedication to the coming murder, but Brutus says that a Roman's word is good enough. He says their task is a virtuous 'enterprise' and that they are all honest men engaged on a 'cause'.

Cassius defers to Brutus

The conspirators discuss who else to involve in the plot. Cicero is put forward as an elder statesman. They think a distinguished older man will give them the credibility and authority their comparative youth lacks. Brutus emphatically rejects the idea, arguing that Cicero would never join in something that he himself did not begin. As soon as Brutus speaks, Cassius and Casca instantly side with him. This shows how quickly Brutus has become the dominant figure in the group.

Alternatively, you should consider whether Cassius – the careful observer of men – may have been right. Cicero's calmness, as witnessed during the storm that terrified Casca, could well have been invaluable.

When Cassius proposes that Mark Antony should also be killed, Brutus argues against it. He says that Antony will be powerless once Caesar is dead and, in any case, he is more interested in enjoying himself at sports and parties. Brutus shows his awareness of the need for restraint. They must be seen to be acting from necessity not hate, to be 'purgers' not 'butchers'. Again Cassius gives way, but his judgement of Mark Antony is a good one; he knows Antony is a 'shrewd contriver' and is 'well beloved of Caesar'. Cassius is afraid that Antony's love of Caesar will make him dangerous after the assassination. Again, Brutus' judgement is questionable.

Sacrifice, not murder

Order, disorder and power

Again, notice how Brutus chooses words to make murder sound like a noble and honourable deed. He tries to make the murder sound like a sort of religious ceremony, almost a holy act. He says the conspirators should be 'sacrificers, but not butchers', they should 'carve him as a dish fit for the gods, not hew him as a carcass fit for hounds'.

Words are powerful things and Brutus is concerned that the 'right' words are used to describe their deeds. This is an important idea in the play: at various times the power of words actually does make things change.

The character of Brutus

Brutus could simply be choosing his words carefully to justify his bloody deed and to make himself look innocent and noble. Or he could be saying that he would like to be able to kill Caesar's spirit but not the man, although this is not possible, of course. Later you will see how Caesar's spirit lives on after his death. How you judge Brutus' character will determine which view you take of him, but both views can be defended by reference to the text.

Fate and the supernatural

The clock strikes three and Cassius wonders whether the strange storm during the night will put Caesar off going to the Capitol that day. He says that Caesar has grown superstitious lately. Decius undertakes to bring Caesar to the Capitol, explaining that although Caesar says he hates flatterers, he is in fact very susceptible to flattery himself. They agree to meet later that morning at eight o'clock at Caesar's house, to escort him to the Capitol.

And now Caius Ligarius

As a final thought Metellus mentions the possibility of including in their group Caius Ligarius, who he says was 'rated' ('berated', or harshly scolded) by Caesar for speaking well of Pompey. The only reason given for including Ligarus is that he 'doth bear Caesar hard', meaning that he regards him as his enemy. Brutus agrees to the suggestion and asks Metellus to send Caius to him, so that he can persuade him.

'Look fresh and merrily'

Order, disorder and power

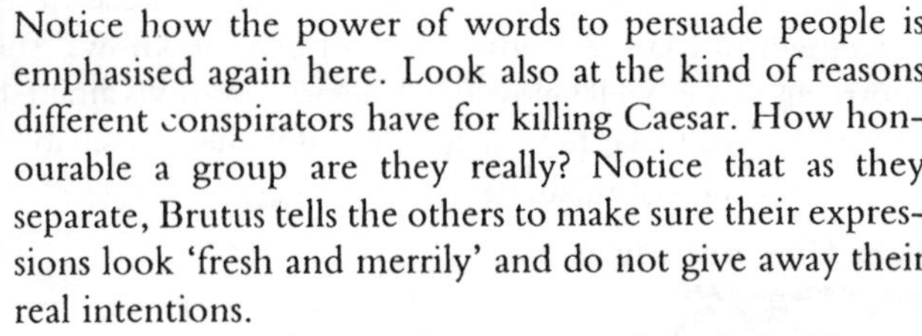

Notice how the power of words to persuade people is emphasised again here. Look also at the kind of reasons different conspirators have for killing Caesar. How honourable a group are they really? Notice that as they separate, Brutus tells the others to make sure their expressions look 'fresh and merrily' and do not give away their real intentions.

Brutus is left alone and sees Lucius fast asleep. He says that unlike him, Lucius has no 'figures or fantasies' to worry him. His wife Portia enters and Brutus gently tells her off for being out in the cold morning and risking her health. You can see that Brutus has up to now had a happy and normal life. Portia and Lucius contrast strongly with the world that Brutus has entered.

Portia is worried about Brutus

Portia is one of the only two women in the play. She is worried about her husband and begs him to tell her what has been on his mind of late. He has not been sleeping or eating, he has been impatient and angry and is clearly disturbed about something. She is worried that he has not responded to all her attempts to share his worries. Brutus tries to pretend to her that it is only because he is not well, but Portia sees through this excuse. She points out that, if he were ill, he would hardly be walking about thinly clothed in the dangerous mists of the cold morning. She seems to suspect a lot of what is going on and is clearly an intelligent and observant person who knows Brutus well. She speaks more revealingly than she perhaps knows when she tells him that if he is sick it is a 'sick offence within your mind'.

Portia accuses Brutus of treating her as less than a true wife, because he will not confide in her. She says she has the stomach for any of his secrets and has deliberately wounded herself in the thigh to demonstrate the strength of her character. They are interrupted by a knocking at the gate. He says he will tell her everything later. As when Brutus never got to the light in his room, the symbolism of this may be that he again turns away from what is good and wholesome towards what is dark and disreputable. Try to decide whether Brutus is here being considerate in protecting his wife from the truth, or whether he is being dishonest and uncaring towards her.

Caius Ligarius arrives

The arrival of Caius Ligarius interrupts the conversation between Brutus and Portia. It says a lot about the power of Brutus' reputation that Ligarius is happy to follow him 'to do I know not what'. Equally it seems that Ligarius is miraculously healed of his illness by 'any exploit worthy of the name of honour'.

'A piece of work that will make sick men whole'

You may see this as a suggestion that the conspirators, by killing Caesar in the name of honour, are going to perform a deed that will cure Rome of the 'sickness' that Cassius thinks it suffers from. In support of this, notice how, when Ligarius asks what it is they are going to do, Brutus says that it is something 'that will make sick men whole'.

Notice too how Brutus carefully avoids naming the act of murder in reply to Ligarius' question 'but are not some whole that we must make sick?'

Honourable or dishonourable men?

Order, disorder and power

Like the others, Ligarius bows to the judgement and leadership of Brutus. Are the conspirators any better than the common people they criticise for blindly following Caesar? You could conclude that the conspirators have given up any real responsibility for what they are doing and have not used their own judgement. In this case you might also feel that the conspiracy is like a sickness that spreads every time someone else joins it.

You might suspect that the conspirators actually rise against Caesar for their own personal and petty reasons. You are not told why some of the conspirators are involved, except that Cassius says he has persuaded them to join him. You might feel, however, that Cassius is involved only because he is jealous of Caesar, Brutus because he feels it is expected of him as an 'honourable' (but vain) man, Casca because he is easily frightened and led, and Ligarius because he hates Caesar for rebuking him.

Act 2 Scene 2

Terrible omens have been seen. Caesar's wife Calphurnia tries to make him stay at home. Caesar reluctantly agrees but Decius arrives and persuades him to go.

It is the Ides of March and the last scene closed, as this one opens, with thunder. This reminds the audience that the heavens are disturbed by events on earth. The action has moved from the house of Brutus to the house of

Caesar. Caesar says that his wife Calphurnia woke up three times in the night crying out that people were murdering him. Caesar sends a servant to tell the priests to make a sacrifice and tell him what the omens are. This reinforces our impressions of Caesar as a privately superstitious man.

Caesar must not go out today

Fate and the supernatural

Calphurnia enters and says Caesar must not go out today. He says he will go out and face danger resolutely, but she persists. She says she is frightened by what has been seen by the night watch; a lioness gave birth in the streets, the dead have risen from their graves, visions of 'fiery warriors' have been seen in the clouds, which themselves rained blood on the Capitol building. She says that the sky has been filled with 'the noises of battle', dying men have groaned and ghosts have shrieked in the streets.

'When beggars die, there are no comets seen; The heavens themselves blaze forth the death of princes.'

Order, disorder and power

Caesar tries to argue that these omens are not meant just for him but are directed at the whole world. Calphurnia echoes the commonly held opinion of Shakespeare's time when she reminds Caesar that strange events in heaven are related to the fates of rulers, princes and kings, not to those of ordinary men.

'Cowards die many times before their deaths; The valiant never taste of death but once.'

Caesar remains unmoved by Calphurnia's arguments and says that brave people only die once, whilst cowards live their lives in constant terror of death. At this point the messenger returns from the priests to say that the omens are bad: one of the creatures they sacrificed was found to have no heart. Caesar immediately interprets this to mean that he would be a creature without a heart – a coward – if he stayed at home because he was afraid to go out. The word 'sacrifice' should remind you of what Brutus said to the other conspirators; that Caesar should be sacrificed, not butchered. In fact they do butcher him like a hunted animal, as Mark Antony later argues to the common people.

Caesar decides he will not go to the Capitol

Finally, Calphurnia succeeds in persuading Caesar to stay at home by saying it is her fear and not his that keeps him in. She says that Mark Antony can go to the Senate House and tell them that Caesar is ill. Although Caesar has so far been defiant, notice how quickly he agrees to this suggestion. You could conclude that he has been looking for some excuse that will not make him look weak, or you might feel that you have seen another side of Caesar. Caesar, a powerful ruler in public, is in private a loving husband who is persuaded to change his mind to save his wife distress.

Caesar decides he will go to the Capitol after all

When Decius arrives Caesar tells him that he will not come to the Senate House today. When asked for a reason, Caesar says he will give none, except that he has decided not to go and that should be reason enough. Caesar is anxious to appear decisive because he fears that his public image will suffer if he admitted that he defers to his wife's demands.

How Decius persuades Caesar

Fate and the supernatural

Decius cleverly asks Caesar for some reason, so that when he tells the Senate that Caesar will not come, they will not laugh at him. The subtle suggestion is that the Senate will laugh at Caesar. Caesar says he will tell Decius the real reason because of his regard for him, although you may suspect that Caesar does not want Decius to think he is being contemptuous towards the Senators. Equally, Caesar may not be able to stomach the idea of people laughing at him. He says Calphurnia has had a dream in which Caesar's statue was running with blood in which smiling Romans bathed their hands. This is of course a vision of the future and by introducing it here Shakespeare heightens the dramatic tension. It is a reminder to the audience, who know how the story comes out, of what is about to happen, but the character of Caesar in the play is ignorant of the dream's real meaning. Caesar's confession gives Decius the opportunity he needs. Decius says that Caesar has misunderstood the meaning of Calphurnia's dream.

Decius interprets Calphurnia's dream to Caesar

Throughout the play you see characters using words and persuasion to manipulate others. Here is another good example. Decius quickly invents another interpretation for the dream, claiming it as a vision of the future, an omen of what has been planned for Caesar. The dream is not a bad sign but a good one, he says. He says it shows how all of Rome draws its strength and health from Caesar. Through Caesar, says Decius, all Romans shall be revived.

Julius Caesar

Decius has already said that Caesar loves to be flattered and that he knows how to manipulate him and it would appear that he was correct. Caesar is immediately convinced by Decius's interpretation, so Decius presses home his advantage. He appeals to Caesar's ambition by saying that he knows the Senate intends to make Caesar king today. If Caesar fails to go they may change their minds, thinking him too easily frightened by his wife's bad dreams. The ploy works and Caesar says he feels ashamed that he listened to his wife's fears. He decides at once to go to the Senate House.

The conspirators arrive

Publius arrives with the assassins to escort Caesar to the Senate. They are joined by Mark Antony. Notice how polite and kind Caesar is towards them. True, he does not know their intentions, but this is a side of him you have not been shown before. Possibly Shakespeare is pointing up the more favourable side of Caesar's character as a contrast to the brutality of his coming murder. More examples of dramatic irony occur when Caesar tells Trebonius to stay near him and invites them all to drink some wine with him 'like friends'. The drinking of wine shows Caesar as a hospitable man but could also be connected – as a symbol – with the 'sacrifice' of Caesar to come.

Friendship

Trebonius remarks in one aside (a comment made to the audience alone) that he will stay so close to Caesar that Caesar's friend will wish he had been further away; Brutus, in another aside, remarks that they may behave 'like' friends, but they are not.

Act 2 Scene 3

The letter from Artemidorus

In this very brief scene Artemidorus reads out a letter which he has written to Caesar. It names the conspirators and warns Caesar to beware of them, for they mean to kill him. Artemidorus says he will give the letter to Caesar as he passes by. If Caesar reads it he will be saved; if he does not, then he will be killed. Notice that Artemidorus has a very different view of Caesar to that of the conspirators. Different characters have different views of Caesar and this reminds you that there is no one final judgement on him. Shakespeare does not allow you to see the issues as black or white, or simply right or wrong. There is as much evidence for Caesar to be seen as a potential tyrant needing to be removed, as for him to be seen as a strong leader with the people's interests at heart, whose murder would be a terrible crime.

Artemidorus says that it is a pity that 'virtue cannot live out of the teeth of emulation', meaning that it is a pity that a virtuous man like Caesar cannot live beyond the reach ('out of the teeth') of those who are his jealous rivals

– those who want to 'emulate' (be like) Caesar. You will remember that Caesar said that Cassius was jealous of those who were greater than himself.

You are not told how Artemidorus came by his information. He seems to know not just who the conspirators are but also why they are in the plot against Caesar and what their different tasks are. This information suggests either that the plot is not as secret as the conspirators think, or that one of them is the source of the information. Whichever is correct, the result is the same; this scene increases the tension in the play by introducing the possibility that Caesar will discover the plot in time to save himself.

Act 2 Scene 4

Portia is worried about Brutus. The soothsayer hopes to warn Caesar of danger. Portia sends Lucius on a strange errand.

Sc 3 and Sc 4 are both very short. They provide an interlude between Caesar leaving his house and arriving at the Senate, during which Shakespeare increases the tension leading up to the fateful murder. He does this by introducing various characters – Artemidorus, Portia and the Soothsayer – who all have some knowledge or premonition of the dreadful events to come.

Portia

Here you see Portia ordering Lucius more than once to run an errand but neglecting to tell him what it is. This indicates the extent of her confusion and emotional turmoil. This is emphasised by the way she speaks in short lines, cannot be still and is frightened by imagined noises. Eventually she sends Lucius to tell Brutus that she is well, to send him her love and to bring back his answer.

Fate and the supernatural

The soothsayer arrives and says that he will wait for Caesar in a wider part of the street so that he might stand a better chance of speaking to him. He says that he has a feeling that Caesar is in danger and he fears that some harm may come to him. Although he does not mention any specific danger, you should remember that it is the Ides of March and the soothsayer told Caesar earlier in the play to beware. His appearance at this moment therefore increases Portia's fears. She and the audience may wonder whether Caesar will read Artemidorus' letter; will the soothsayer reach him in time?

Portia

Portia cannot stand the strain any longer and says she must go in. You could conclude from this scene that Brutus has told her the details of the plot and this is why she is so agitated. There is evidence in support of this when Portia says that she hopes the heavens will speed Brutus in his 'enterprise'. Interestingly, this is the same word Brutus used to describe the plot. Also, she appears to be trying to cover up what she sees as a mistake, when she realises that Lucius has heard her and says, by way of explanation, that she meant that Brutus has asked Caesar for a request ('a suit') that Caesar is reluctant to agree to.

This Act features **domestic scenes** in the houses of Brutus and Caesar. **Caesar and Brutus** are in many ways alike and it is not easy to know which of them is better or more unscrupulous than the other. Both have weaknesses and are susceptible to being flattered and manipulated by others. Both appear to have caring and loving wives and happy home backgrounds. Both in their different ways could be seen as ambitious and at times arrogant. Both make fatal mistakes of judgement about others. Both read omens and signs in a way that favours their own cause. Both have public images of themselves that they feel they have to live up to but in their private lives both are kind, loving and wracked by doubts and fears. Both men also have great qualities as leaders of others.

Brutus has only his fears of what Caesar may become to justify the assassination. Images of **light and dark** and the innocence of youth are used to emphasise how these fears and the conspiracy are leading him away from peace and happiness and are depriving him of sleep and his peace of mind. Imagery of **blood, fire and storm** is used, as it is in the rest of the play, to underline the way the forces of nature are signalling that chaos and destruction in the world are already present. Characters interpret these images in different ways, to suit their own purposes. This is also true of the interpretation given to other omens, e.g. Calphurnia's dreams and the priests' sacrifices.

The importance of language is emphasised. Brutus is anxious that the conspirators' deeds are seen by the common people as 'necessary' and 'noble'. Caesar is anxious that he is not seen by the senators to be 'frightened' by evil omens. Words and the way others will 'speak of' their deeds are important to many of the characters.

Self-test (Questions) Act Two

Uncover the plot

Delete two of the three alternatives given, to find the correct plot. Beware possible misconceptions and muddles.

Cicero/Brutus/Lucius agrees to join the conspirators in their plot to murder Antony/Caesar/Octavius, but refuses to drink wine/plan the murder/take an oath of allegiance with them. They mean to petition/assassinate/imprison Caesar when he goes to the Capitol that day. Brutus' wife Flavia/Calpurnia/Portia comes to him worried about his indigestion/sleeplessness/rheumatism, but he does not tell her about the plot. Meanwhile, Caesar's wife Livia/Portia/Calphurnia tells him of 'horrid sights' seen by the watchmen that night and tries to persuade him to stay at home. Caesar refuses/agrees/is undecided. But when Decius comes to accompany Caesar to the Capitol, he agrees with Calphurnia/suggests Caesar stays at home/changes Caesar's mind. Artemidorus/Trebonius/Dardanus writes a letter to Caesar, warning him of the omens/weather/conspiracy. Portia, worried about Brutus, sends his servant Strato/Clitus/Lucius to give her report of what Brutus says and how he looks. A tribune/soothsayer/priest also goes to the Capitol to warn Caesar again that he is in danger.

Why? What? Who?

1 Why does Brutus fear Caesar becoming king?
2 What does Lucius find on Brutus' window sill?
3 Who comes to Brutus' house to plot the assassination?
4 Who does Cassius want to join the plot?
5 Who is given to 'sports, wildness and much company'?
6 What has Portia done to prove her strength of character?
7 What bad news do the priests give Caesar?
8 Why does Portia fear for Brutus at the Capitol?
9 What does the soothsayer say will happen at the Capitol that day?
10 What does Portia say to Lucius is her husband's 'enterprise'?

Who said that?

1 Who said: 'I know no other cause to spurn at him,/But for the general.'
2 Who said: 'But 'tis a common proof,/That lowliness is young ambition's ladder'
3 Who said: 'what other oath/Than honesty to honesty engaged'
4 Who said: 'Seeing that death, a necessary end,/ Will come when it will come'
5 Who said: 'If thou read this, O Caesar, thou mayst live;/If not, the Fates with traitors do contrive.'

Open quotes

Find the line – and complete the phrase or sentence.

1 'When beggars die, there are no comets seen...'
2 'Cowards die many times...'
3 'It is the bright day that brings...'
4 'Let's carve him as a dish...'
5 'Caesar should be a beast...'

Prove it!

Find a quote from the text that could be used to back up each of the following statements.

1 Brutus has had trouble sleeping.
2 Caesar is not afraid of death.
3 Decius has great affection for Caesar.

On the other hand...

Find a quote from the text that could be used to argue against each of the following.

1 Brutus believes Antony is powerful in his own right.
2 Brutus thinks Antony is a quiet, responsible man.
3 Caesar has not become superstitious.

In time

Three people ask the time during this Act. Who are they and what are the answers?

Reversals

Find three instances of people saying that things are other than they seem.

The storm continues

Calpurnia reports 'horrid sights seen by the watch'. Find FOUR quotes which match her description to that given by Casca in Act1 Sc3.

Self-test (Answers) Act Two

Uncover the plot

Brutus agrees to join the conspirators in their plot to murder Caesar, but refuses to take an oath of allegiance with them. They mean to assassinate Caesar when he goes to the Capitol that day. Brutus' wife Portia comes to him worried about his sleeplessness, but he does not tell her about the plot. Meanwhile, Caesar's wife Calphurnia tells him of 'horrid sights' seen by the watchmen that night and tries to persuade him to stay at home. Caesar agrees. But when Decius comes to accompany Caesar to the Capitol, he changes Caesar's mind. Artemidorus writes a letter to Caesar, warning him of the conspiracy. Portia, worried about Brutus, sends his servant Lucius to give her report of what Brutus says and how he looks. A soothsayer also goes to the Capitol to warn Caesar again that he is in danger.

Why? What? Who?

1 He is afraid that Caesar will become a tyrant and abuse his power
2 A letter encouraging Brutus to take action against Caesar
3 Cassius, Casca, Decius Brutus, Cinna, Metellus Cimber and Trebonius
4 Cicero
5 Antony
6 She has deliberately wounded herself in the thigh
7 They sacrificed an animal and found it had no heart – a bad omen
8 She is worried about his health
9 He says he does not know what will happen, but fears what may happen
10 That Brutus has a petition which Caesar refuses to grant

Who said that?

1 Brutus 2,1
2 Brutus 2,1
3 Brutus 2,1
4 Caesar 2,2
5 Artemidorus 2,3

Open quotes

1 'When beggars die, there are no comets seen;/The heavens themselves blaze forth the death of princes.' 2,2
2 'Cowards die many times before their deaths;/ the valiant never taste of death but once.' 2,2
3 'It is the bright day that brings forth the adder;/And that craves wary walking.' 2,1'
4 'Let's carve him as a dish fit for the gods,/Not hew him as a carcass fit for hounds'2,1
5 'Caesar should be a beast without a heart,/If he should stay at home today for fear.' 2,2

Prove it!

1 'You've ungently, Brutus,/Stole from my bed: and yesternight at supper,/ You suddenly arose, and walk'd about.' 2,1
2 'death, a necessary end,/Will come when it will come' 2,2
3 'Pardon me, Caesar, for my dear dear love/To your proceeding bids me tell you this;' 2,2

On the other hand...

1 'For Antony is but a limb of Caesar' 2,1
2 'for he is given/To sports, to wildness and much company.' 2,1
3 'For he is superstitious grown of late,/Quite from the main opinion he held once' 2,1

In time

1 Brutus; it is 3 a.m. 2,1
2 Caesar; it is 8 a.m. 2,2
3 Portia; it is 9 a.m. 2,4

Reversals

1 Decius says Caesar can be flattered 2,1
2 Decius reinterprets Calphurnia's dream 2,2
3 Portia says Brutus' 'enterprise' is a 'suit that Caesar will not grant' 2,2

The storm continues

1 'A lioness hath whelped in the streets' 2,2
'Against the Capitol I met a lion' 1,3
2 'Graves hath yawned and yielded up their dead' 2,2
'there were drawn/Upon a heap a hundred ghastly women' 1,3
3 'Fierce fiery warriors fought upon the clouds' 2,2
'Men all in fire walk up and down the streets' 1,3
4 'Horses did neigh and dying men did groan' 2,2
'The bird of night did sit... hooting and shrieking' 1,3

Act 3 Scene 1

Caesar is assassinated. Antony offers to make peace with the conspirators and Brutus agrees. Antony privately vows revenge for Caesar's murder.

Caesar misses two chances to save himself

Caesar has arrived with his companions outside the Senate house. Seeing the soothsayer in the crowd, he jokes that the Ides of March have arrived. The soothsayer replies that he is right, but that the day is not yet over. Artemidorus interrupts and presses Caesar to read the message he gives him. Decius quickly steps in with a diversion – a suit (request) from Trebonius. Notice how Decius is more polite than Artemidorus who urges Caesar to read his letter first because it is of more personal interest to him – it 'touches Caesar nearer' as he puts it. When Artemidorus becomes insistent, Caesar rebuffs him and loses his last chance to save his life.

Did Caesar have any real choice?

Fate and the supernatural

Ironically, by not putting his own interests first, Caesar has prevented himself from discovering the conspiracy. If Caesar had behaved in a more selfish way he may have been saved. You may think Caesar is just pretending to think about himself last because he is a clever politician. On the other hand, if you feel that Caesar is an honest and noble man, you may see this and the refusal of the crown as genuinely modest and statesmanlike acts.

The tension increases

Whichever view of Caesar you take, notice how Shakespeare increases the dramatic tension with this meeting of Caesar, the soothsayer and Artemidorus.

The conspirators' secret is out

Order, disorder and power

The tension increases further when Popilius Lena approaches Cassius saying, 'I wish your enterprise today may thrive'. Cassius panics because it is clear that more people know about the plot than the conspirators thought. Brutus reassures Cassius that Popilius is chatting and smiling and that Caesar's behaviour does not alter. Other events seem to be going to plan, as Trebonius draws Mark Antony away from Caesar, so that he will not be able to intervene.

Metellus Cimber pleads for his brother

As the conspirators begin to close in on Caesar, Cinna tells Casca that he is to strike the first blow. It has been arranged that Metellus Cimber will put his request ('prefer his suit') to Caesar. His suit concerns his banished brother

Publius Cimber. Metellus tries to flatter Caesar by kneeling, calling him 'most high, most mighty' and stressing his own 'humble heart'. Caesar is annoyed by this obvious attempt to flatter him, perhaps even more annoyed by the suggestion that he can be so easily swayed.

Caesar cannot be persuaded

Caesar says he is immune to the things that might sway fools, children or ordinary men, such as flattery, bowing and scraping and 'base spaniel fawning'. If Metellus wants Caesar to overrule the banishment, he must give him proper reasons and cause to do so because 'Caesar doth not wrong'. Metellus asks whether Caesar would relent if someone more worthy than himself were to beg for his brother's return. Brutus kisses Caesar's hand, then Cassius kneels before him, both begging in exaggerated humility that Publius's sentence be repealed.

Why Caesar will not change his mind

Friendship

Try to decide whether Caesar's refusal to be flattered, or to change the law because his friends ask him a favour shows he is a strong and courageous ruler who has deep convictions and respect for the law, or whether he refuses to change his mind because he thinks it will make him look weak. Is Caesar being unfeeling and arrogant? Look carefully at the last speech he makes before he is murdered.

Order, disorder and power

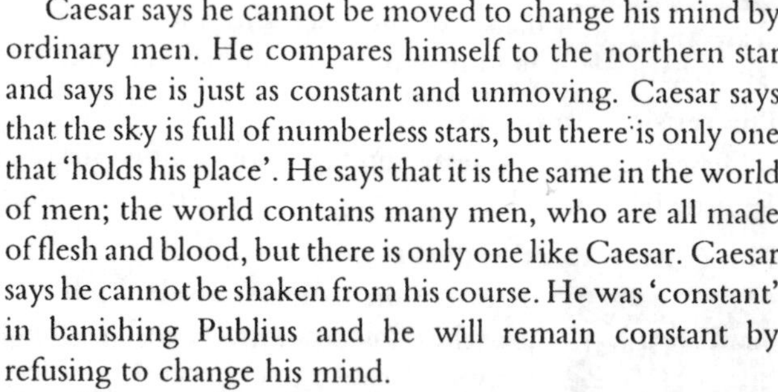

Caesar says he cannot be moved to change his mind by ordinary men. He compares himself to the northern star and says he is just as constant and unmoving. Caesar says that the sky is full of numberless stars, but there is only one that 'holds his place'. He says that it is the same in the world of men; the world contains many men, who are all made of flesh and blood, but there is only one like Caesar. Caesar says he cannot be shaken from his course. He was 'constant' in banishing Publius and he will remain constant by refusing to change his mind.

Depending on the view you take of Caesar, you may see this speech as a statement of how strongly he holds to his principles, or as the ravings of a callous tyrant.

Friendship

'Et tu, Brute?'

The conspirators stab Caesar one by one, until he falls dead. Caesar's only words are 'Et tu, Brute?', meaning 'You too, Brutus?', and you are not told whether Caesar is surprised or saddened to see someone whom he thought his close friend involved in the murder.

Panic breaks out

Immediately after the murder the conspirators cry out that tyranny is dead and that they have acted for freedom and liberty. They are elated and frightened at the same time, and the surrounding senators seem stunned by what has happened. Cassius knows how important it is to get immediate control of the streets and he organises the rest to do this. Trebonius enters with the news that Mark Antony has fled to his house and that there is panic in the streets.

Brutus says that what is to happen next is in the hands of fate; whether they are themselves to die for what they have done is unclear. The conspirators seem to have no real idea of what to do next. Brutus assumes that the people will see the murder in the same way that he does and will understand the justice of it. Compare this turmoil with the careful planning shown later in the play by Antony.

The murderers bathe their hands in Caesar's blood

Brutus tells the others to bathe their hands up to the elbows with the blood of Caesar, smear it on their swords, and walk through the streets shouting 'Peace, freedom, and liberty!' Notice that he assumes that the population will understand this action without explanation. This action fits in with what Brutus said earlier in the play about treating Caesar's murder as a religious sacrifice.

Fate and the supernatural

Notice that Brutus' instructions echo the dream of Calphurnia, in which Caesar said:

> '...my statue,
> Which, like a fountain with an hundred spouts,
> Did run pure blood; and many lusty Romans
> Came smiling, and did bathe their hands in it.'

It also echoes the vision of the women earlier during the storm: 'Men, all in fire, walk up and down the streets.'

What will people in the future think?

Cassius and Brutus wonder how many times in the future their deeds will be the subject of plays. Cassius says that every time they are portrayed, people will remember how they gave their country liberty. This may be ironic, since Shakespeare has taken care to remain impartial and the audience may not see the conspirators in this way at all.

Cassius seems happy to let Brutus lead the way through the streets. This may be an example of Cassius following Brutus as the group's leader or it could be an example of Cassius continuing to manipulate Brutus by letting him think he is really in control.

Mark Antony sends a message

At this point the action of the play changes direction as a servant of Mark Antony's arrives with a message. Up to now you have seen very little of Antony. The arrival of a message from him – rather than his arrival in person – prepares the ground for his emergence as an important character. The servant says that he has been told to kneel before Brutus and give him a message from Antony.

Antony's message acknowledges those features of Brutus's character that Brutus himself values; nobility, wisdom, bravery, honesty. It then mentions features of Caesar's character which the conspirators are unlikely to object to, saying he was 'mighty, bold, royal and loving'. Antony is careful to list these characteristics as though they were simple facts.

Antony asks why Caesar deserved to die

Antony says that he loves and honours Brutus. Notice how he says the same about Caesar, except that he also 'feared' Caesar. This is not necessarily a criticism of Caesar, although he may be assuming that Brutus will see it as one. Antony says that if Brutus will guarantee his safety, he will come to Brutus to learn why Caesar has been killed. If Brutus can tell him why Caesar truly

deserved to die, then Antony will love the living Brutus more than the dead Caesar and will become his follower. Antony takes care to make sure that the ground is safe before he meets the conspirators. His careful planning and preparation contrasts with the way the conspirators have let their plans become known in advance and given little thought to what they would do after Caesar's murder.

Brutus again ignores the suspicions of Cassius

Friendship

Brutus is persuaded by Antony's rational appeal and tells the servant to ask Antony to come. You may think that Antony has read the character of Brutus well and knows how to appeal successfully to him. Brutus already seems disposed to accept Antony as a friend. Cassius says he does not trust Antony, but there is no time for the discussion to develop, as Mark Antony enters at this point.

Antony arrives in person

Antony speaks in praise of the dead Caesar, then turns to the conspirators and says that he does not know what they intend to do next, but offers them his life there and then, saying that if they intend to kill him now is a perfect time.

Antony may be being very cunning here. He is certainly playing for high stakes in offering them his life. He may have calculated that they will be satisfied with one murder, or it could be that since the plot was not well concealed, he already knows of their decision not to harm him. It is difficult to decide how much of a real risk Antony is running here, or whether he is so grief-stricken that he genuinely does not care whether they kill him or not. Remember that he established through his servant that it was safe for him to appear. Whatever Antony's real motives, he makes a shrewd move in what he does here, because he forces Brutus to guarantee his safety.

Brutus says that although they must appear to be 'bloody and cruel', they killed Caesar only because they felt there was no other way to save Rome. Brutus assures Antony that he is safe from harm.

Antony is invited to join the conspirators

Cassius says they want Antony to join them in deciding which people will have positions and honours in the new government. Remember that Cassius does not trust Antony and see if you can decide why he should want Antony to be seen to be so publicly involved in events after the murder. Cassius is actually offering Antony a subtle bribe – a share of political power. Think about how this would appear to the common working people of Rome and notice that Antony carefully does not answer. Antony seems to know that although Cassius does not trust him, he is a clever political manipulator, but he also knows that Brutus is driven by considerations of 'honour'. He knows it is important not to arouse Brutus' suspicions by appearing to lack honourable motives.

Brutus says Antony should wait until things are calm again. He will then explain why he, who loved Caesar so much, had to kill him.

'I doubt not of your wisdom'

Antony now makes a long and important speech. He begins by saying that he does not doubt that the conspirators are wise: 'I doubt not of your wisdom'. This is a very carefully worded phrase. He says nothing about their *actions* or their *judgement*, only that they are wise men. The conspirators will assume that he means they have *acted* wisely by killing Caesar and will therefore feel reassured that Antony is on their side, but this is not what he actually says. You will have to decide what you think Antony means.

Friendship

Antony deliberately shakes hands with each of the conspirators in turn. He then turns to the matter of what the conspirators must now think of him, saying that they must see him as either a coward or a flatterer but either way they must think badly of him. He says that it is true that he loved and respected Caesar. Antony begs forgiveness of Caesar's ghost. Look carefully at how Antony describes Caesar's death: he says Caesar was 'bayed' like a 'brave hart'. He describes Caesar as though he were a noble, free and beautiful deer which has been hunted and struck down. When Cassius interrupts him he asks Cassius's pardon, saying that even Caesar's enemies would say as much about him.

Cassius does not blame Antony for praising Caesar; he interrupted Antony because he wants to know what kind of relationship Antony wants with them; will he become their ally, or should they pass him by and not depend on his support?

Mark Antony

Antony tells the conspirators that if he is to be their ally they must tell him why Caesar was so dangerous. Brutus promises that they will give him reasons good enough to convince even a son of Caesar. This may be only a manner of speaking on the part of Brutus but this kind of thinking does seem typical of him. He assumes that giving a person a good reason is all that is needed to persuade them. Does Brutus overestimate the influence of reason and logic over people's behaviour and underestimate the power of people's emotions?

Antony wishes to speak at Caesar's funeral

Caius Cassius

Antony makes what seems like an innocent request when he asks if he may, as a friend of Caesar's, speak at his funeral. Brutus agrees, but immediately Cassius calls him to one side to speak to him. Cassius is aware that Antony may move the people by what he says and is worried about the possible consequences. Brutus feels confident because he will speak first and will show 'the reason of our Caesar's death'. Brutus is sure that it will be of benefit to their cause in the eyes of the people if they see that Antony is allowed to speak at Caesar's funeral, because Caesar will then have been given 'all true rites and lawful ceremonies'. Again, Brutus assumes that people are persuaded by reason, not emotion. Cassius still seems to be the practical thinker but allows himself to be persuaded by Brutus, who imagines that, by dictating the content of Antony's speech, he can prevent him from saying anything dangerous.

Marcus Brutus

'Let slip the dogs of war'

Fate and the supernatural

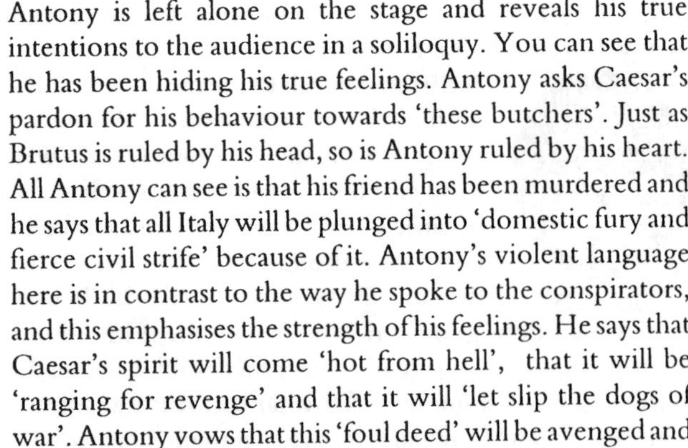

Antony is left alone on the stage and reveals his true intentions to the audience in a soliloquy. You can see that he has been hiding his true feelings. Antony asks Caesar's pardon for his behaviour towards 'these butchers'. Just as Brutus is ruled by his head, so is Antony ruled by his heart. All Antony can see is that his friend has been murdered and he says that all Italy will be plunged into 'domestic fury and fierce civil strife' because of it. Antony's violent language here is in contrast to the way he spoke to the conspirators, and this emphasises the strength of his feelings. He says that Caesar's spirit will come 'hot from hell', that it will be 'ranging for revenge' and that it will 'let slip the dogs of war'. Antony vows that this 'foul deed' will be avenged and from now on he will become Caesar's avenging spirit.

Antony weeps when Octavius' servant comes in and recoils from the sight of Caesar's body. The servant tells him that Octavius is coming to Rome. Antony says that he will take Caesar's body into the market place to speak to the people about the 'cruel issue of these bloody men'. Octavius must stay outside Rome until he knows the outcome of Antony's speech to the people.

In Shakespeare's time, the figure of a ghost looking for revenge was common in plays. Here you can see the introduction of a 'character' to replace the living Caesar; the spirit of Caesar.

Act 3 Scene 2

Brutus and Antony make their speeches in the marketplace.

Brutus arrives in the marketplace to tell the people why the conspirators acted as they did. Cassius goes off elsewhere to do the same. The common working people split up, some going to Brutus and some to Cassius. One of the citizens says he will go with Cassius and meet his friend later to compare what he hears with what Brutus says. This suggests that the people will want to be sure that all the conspirators give a fair and truthful account.

Who should the people believe?

You should carefully compare the speech of Brutus with that of Antony. Brutus asks rhetorical questions in his speech – questions that he does not really expect anyone to answer – because there is only one response. For example, he asks them if they would rather Caesar were alive and they all 'die as slaves', or whether they would rather be free, with Caesar dead. Put this way there is only one answer. This is what Brutus does when he asks the crowd if there is anyone 'so vile' that they will not love their country.

Brutus appeals to the crowd's reason by arguing cleverly with words. Brutus says that because Caesar loved him he weeps for his death; when Caesar was fortunate he was happy for him; because he was valiant he honours him; but because Caesar was ambitious he killed him. Brutus makes it sound as though he had no choice in the matter and as though Caesar brought his death upon himself. Brutus finishes by offering to lay down his own life if his country needs it.

Brutus appears to have been very successful, because the crowd are clearly persuaded by his arguments. How far has Brutus manipulated their thinking with his speech? How far they are genuinely persuaded might be indicated by the way they react to Antony's speech. You might feel that the common people will follow whoever last spoke to them.

'Friends, Romans, countrymen, lend me your ears;
I come to bury Caesar, not to praise him.'

Antony talks to the people as an ordinary person speaking to them individually. He claims he is not a great speaker, only a blunt and straightforward man. Unlike Brutus, Antony uses language to arouse emotions, not to try and persuade with logic. Every word in Antony's speech is carefully calculated to stir up the crowd's emotions. It is a brilliant piece of oratory, perfectly thought out from beginning to end. It is ironic that after his first speech the initial response from the crowd is that there is much 'reason' (meaning 'truth') in what Antony has said.

'The evil that men do lives after them,
The good is oft interred with their bones'

Antony says that when people die their good deeds and qualities are often forgotten whilst their sins are remembered. He says that Caesar's murderers are 'honourable' men, but repeats it so often and in such a way that the crowd understand that he means the opposite. He carefully says that he has not come to disprove what Brutus said but only to 'speak what I do know'. This 'direct and honest' approach proves very effective.

'My heart is in the coffin there with Caesar,
And I must pause till it come back to me.'

Antony offers the crowd several examples of Caesar's behaviour from which they may judge his character: he brought captured wealth back to Rome which benefited everyone; he used to weep when the poor people suffered;

and he refused the crown three times. Antony asks the crowd to consider if these seem like the actions of an ambitious man. He pauses dramatically, saying he is overcome with emotion, before resuming his speech.

Antony brings out Caesar's will

Antony says he will not do Brutus and Cassius wrong by stirring the crowd to 'mutiny and rage' but will instead choose to 'wrong' the dead, himself and them. He has brought Caesar's will with him, but tells the crowd he will not read it out because to do so would make them realise that Caesar was their greatest friend and 'benefactor'.

Antony has cleverly stirred the crowd's feelings and awakened both their curiosity and their greed. He says he will not read the document because it is not proper that they should know how much Caesar loved them.

'You are not wood, you are not stones, but men.'

It is during this speech that the sympathies of the crowd change and the turning-points in the fortunes of the conspirators and Mark Antony are reached. To emphasise this, Shakespeare reverses a line spoken much earlier. At the start of the play Marullus calls the ordinary people 'you blocks, you stones, you worse than senseless things'. Here Antony says 'you are not wood, you are not stones, but men'. Antony's speeches here are effective and powerful because he reaches out to the people's individual human emotions.

'If you have tears, prepare to shed them now.'

Mark Antony

Before he reads them Caesar's will, he insists that they stand in a circle round Caesar's body. He talks about Caesar's cloak, how it accompanied him on all his great victories and how it is now pierced with gashes from the conspirator's swords. Antony may be appealing to the baser instincts of the crowd but, unlike Brutus, he seems convincing – he seems really to believe what he is saying. Antony's speeches seem to come from the heart, whereas Brutus' seemed to come from the head. In fact, both speeches are carefully calculated.

'Revenge! About! Seek! Burn! Fire! Kill! Slay! Let not a traitor live.'

Order, disorder and power

By now the crowd, in a frenzy of emotion, seek revenge at the 'bloody sight'. Antony protests that he does not want to stir them to mutiny, that he is not an orator like Brutus but only 'a plain blunt man, that love my friend'. He says that Caesar's wounds will speak for him and will move the stones of Rome to rise and revolt. Now Antony plays his strongest card. He tells them he will read Caesar's will.

Antony reads Caesar's will

According to Antony, Caesar has left every man some money and has left to all the people his walks, gardens and orchards for their pleasure for ever. The crowd are determined to avenge the death of Caesar and say they will burn Caesar's body 'in the holy place', and then burn the conspirators' houses. As the crowd depart Antony hears news that Brutus and Cassius have heard news of how Antony has stirred up the people against them and have fled the city.

Act 3 Scene 3

The poet Cinna is mistaken for a conspirator and killed.

Order, disorder and power

This scene shows the common people as an unthinking mob. Cinna the poet has had a puzzling dream that he was at a feast with Caesar. He is walking the streets when a mob finds him and questions him. He tells the mob his name and they assume that he is the conspirator Cinna. When he protests that he is Cinna the poet, the mob cries that he should be killed for his bad poetry. They are so enraged that they do not seem to care who he is and they kill him.

This scene shows the effects of Antony's speech. The common people seem to have lost the power of reason. Notice that it is a poet – someone who uses words sensitively and perceptively – who is the innocent victim of their aggression. In this brief scene Shakespeare was not trying to suggest that all ordinary working people are unthinking barbarians. Remember the opening of the play, where the common working people appear as witty and intelligent individuals. Shakespeare is making points about the way the power of language can be used either to encourage people to think and reason sensitively or to encourage unthinking and hysterical hatred and rage.

Caesar is assassinated amidst scenes of high tension, where he is offered but refuses a letter containing details of the murder plot and where the conspirators' 'secret' is shown to be more widely known than they thought. The conspirators – especially Brutus – hope that the common people will understand their actions but their attempt to persuade them is thwarted by a brilliant speech by Antony, who rouses the mob against them.

You do not get a very flattering picture of the **common people** in this Act. The play raises important issues about whether ordinary people really are fit to govern themselves or whether instead they need a wise and strong ruler to have power over them. One view might be that uneducated people are easily led and that their more educated fellow citizens bear much responsibility for leading them properly. Before you conclude that Shakespeare was sometimes unflattering towards the ordinary people of his own time you should ask yourself whether ordinary people today would react all that differently in similar circumstances.

Self-test (Questions) Act Three

Uncover the plot

Delete two of the three alternatives given, to find the correct plot. Beware possible misconceptions and muddles.

On his way to the Forum, Caesar rebuffs/listens to/does not see the soothsayer and Artemidorus, both of whom want to warn him of imminent luck/danger/rain. Then he refuses Marcellus'/Metellus'/Messala's plea to release his brother from banishment. The conspirators crowd round Caesar and stab him, one by one, Cinna/Cassius/Casca first. Afterwards, Antony/Octavius/Lepidus offers to make peace with the assassins, provided he is allowed to speak at Caesar's funeral. Casca is reluctant to allow this, but Brutus hesitates/refuses/agrees – so long as Antony does not blame them. In private, Antony weeps/vows revenge/plans to flee. At the Forum, Brutus speaks to the crowd, insisting that he loved/loathed/was jealous Caesar, but killed him for the good of Rome. Antony then speaks in Caesar's defence, saying he was not ambitious and denounces the conspirators by extravagantly praising their 'honour'/'virtue'/'charity'. He reads from Caesar's will that each Roman has been left 100/75/50 drachmas and the use of Caesar's private grounds. In the uproar which follows, the murderers flee and the singer/actor/poet Cinna is killed because he has the same name as one of the assassins.

Who? Why? Which? Where?

1 Who try to warn Caesar of the danger he is in?
2 Why does Caesar refuse to read Artemidorus' letter – and why is this ironic?
3 Which senator does Casca fear knows about the plot?
4 What does Metellus Cimber want from Caesar?
5 Where do Brutus and Cassius go after Antony's speech?

Open quotes

Find the line – and complete the phrase or sentence.

1 'But I am constant as the northern star...'
2 'Why, he that cuts off twenty years of life...'
3 'Not that I loved Caesar less,...'
4 'Friends, Romans, countrymen, lend me your ears...'
5 'My heart is in the coffin...'

Prove it!

Find a quote from the text that could be used to back up each of the following statements.

1 The conspirators know their deed will go down in history.
2 Antony wants to make peace with the conspirators.
3 Antony says he is a poor orator.

Fill in the blanks

Servant: 'Brutus is ..., ..., valiant, and ...;
Caesar was ..., ..., royal, and ...;
Say I ... Brutus and I honour him
Say I ... Caesar, honour'd him, and ... him.' 3,1

Brutus: 'As Caesar ... me, I weep for him; As he was a ..., I rejoice at it, as he was ..., I honour him; but as he was ..., I slew him.' 3,2

Skilful speakers

Both Brutus and Antony use words to manipulate the crowd's emotions, but Antony is more successful than Brutus.

1 Find ONE way in which the speeches are similar and ONE way in which they are different.
2 During the first part of his speech, Antony repeats one phrase (or a variation of it) seven times. What is the phrase, and what is its effect on the crowd?
3 Brutus uses the speaker's skill of asking rhetorical questions (questions for which no answer is expected) in his speech. Find these, then identify another effect which makes his speech more powerful.

Self-test (Answers) Act Three

Uncover the plot

On his way to the Forum, Caesar rebuffs the soothsayer and Artemidorus, both of whom want to warn him of imminent danger. Then he refuses Metellus' plea to release his brother from banishment. The conspirators crowd round Caesar and stab him, one by one, Casca first. Afterwards, Antony offers to make peace with the assassins, provided he is allowed to speak at Caesar's funeral. Casca is reluctant to allow this, but Brutus agrees – so long as Antony does not blame them. In private, Antony vows revenge. At the Forum, Brutus speaks to the crowd, insisting that he loved Caesar but killed him for the good of Rome. Antony then speaks in Caesar's defence, saying he was not ambitious, and denounces the conspirators by extravagantly praising their 'honour'. He reads from Caesar's will that each Roman has been left 75 drachmas and the use of Caesar's private grounds. In the uproar which follows, the murderers flee and the poet Cinna is killed because he has the same name as one of the assassins.

Who? Why? Which? Where?

1 The soothsayer and Artemidorus
2 Because Artemidorus says it 'touches Caesar nearer', and Caesar wants to put his personal concerns last – ironic in the light of what happens next
3 Popilius Lena
4 To release his brother from banishment
5 They flee the city

Open quotes

1 'But I am constant as the northern star, /Of whose true-fix'd and resting quality/There is no fellow in the firmament' 3,1
2 'Why, he that cuts off twenty years of life/Cuts off so many years of fearing death.'3,1
3 'Not that I loved Caesar less, but that I loved Rome more' 3,2
4 'Friends, Romans, countrymen, lend me your ears;/I come to bury Caesar, not to praise him.'
5 'My heart is in the coffin there with Caesar,/And I must pause till it come back to me' 3,2

Prove it!

1 'How many ages hence/Shall this our lofty scene be acted over' 3,1
2 'Friends, I am with you all and love you all' 3,2
3 'I am no orator, as Brutus is;/But, as you know me all, a plain blunt man' 3,2

Fill in the blanks

Servant: 'Brutus is noble, wise, valiant, and honest;
Caesar was mighty, bold, royal, and loving;
Say I ... Brutus and I honour him
Say I loved Caesar, honour'd him, and ... him.' 3,1

Brutus: 'As Caesar loved me, I weep for him; As he was a fortunate, I rejoice at it, as he was valiant I honour him; but as he was ambitious, I slew him.' 3,2

Skilful speakers

1 Similar: the openings – Brutus: 'Romans, countrymen, and lovers...'; Antony: 'Friends, Romans, countrymen...'. Both appeal to the crowd's patriotism
Different: Brutus' speech is in prose; Antony's in verse
2 'Brutus is an honourable man'/'honourable men'. Antony repeats it so often that the crowd knows he is being sarcastic (Fourth Citizen: 'They were traitors: Honourable men!')
3 'Who is here so base that would be a bondman?', 'Who is here so rude that would not be a Roman?', 'Who is here so vile that will not love his country?' 3,2. Other effect: repetition ('As Caesar... as he... as he'; 'If any, speak... If any, speak... If any, speak' 3,2)

Act 4 Scene 1

Antony, Octavius and Lepidus make a list of their enemies who shall be executed.

Friendship

Antony said that Caesar's spirit would come 'hot from hell', that it will be 'ranging for revenge' and that it will 'let slip the dogs of war'. Here you see him putting this into action. 'These many then shall die', says Antony as the three men make a death-list of those who they dislike. These three are now the triumvirate that governs Rome. They are casual and cold-blooded in making their list. Lepidus agrees that his own brother should die, but only if Antony's nephew Publius dies also. Brother has turned against brother and friend against friend.

Mark Antony

Antony sends Lepidus to get Caesar's will. He wants to 'cut off some charge in legacies' (deprive the people of the money that Caesar left to them). He tells Octavius that Lepidus is 'a slight unmeritable man' who is fit only to be used like a trained animal. Once Lepidus has done what is wanted of him, Antony says they must discard him. Antony shows himself in this scene to be single-minded and determined, prepared to kill, manipulate others and cheat the people to achieve what he wants. Antony is the avenging spirit of Caesar, but is he becoming an evil man, obsessed by revenge for Caesar's murder, or was he always like this?

Antony and Octavius agree to combine forces in order to defeat the enemies that surround them.

Act 4 Scene 2

At the camp near Sardis, Cassius tells Brutus that he thinks he has been badly treated by him.

Marcus Brutus

Lucilius, a follower of Brutus, has returned from Cassius' camp, where he was treated in a polite but not friendly way. Brutus thinks the friendship of Cassius is cooling. Cassius arrives and accuses Brutus of treating him unfairly. Notice how quickly Brutus reacts to this situation. You have seen before that Brutus is a clever person who knows the effect that words and actions have on other people. He denies that he has done Cassius any wrong, but says they should not be seen to quarrel in front of their men because it is bad for morale. They go into Brutus' tent to continue their discussion.

Notice that the action of the play has now shifted away from Rome. The rest of the play is about the defeat and deaths of Brutus and Cassius.

Act 4 Scene 3

Brutus and Cassius quarrel. Brutus tells of Portia's suicide and decides that the army shall march to Philippi. The ghost of Caesar visits Brutus and tells him it will see him again at Philippi.

Caius Cassius

Cassius is angry because Brutus has punished an officer who has taken bribes. Brutus says that rumour has it that Cassius has also taken bribes and accuses him of withholding money that he needed to pay his army. Cassius says he did not refuse the money; the servant who returned with his answer was a fool and must have muddled it up.

Order, disorder and power

Think about where your sympathies lie in this quarrel between Brutus and Cassius. Brutus takes a stand on being honest and uncorrupted, saying that they did not kill Caesar in order to stoop to dishonesty themselves. As a devious political person, Cassius thinks a certain amount of corruption acceptable to get the result that is wanted. Brutus refuses to accept this, saying that they killed Caesar because he abused his power and that they must not go the same way or they will be no better than him. But Brutus is not above asking Cassius for money, even though he condemns the way it has been obtained. There is perhaps a certain amount of muddled thinking here by Brutus, just as there was about his own 'honour' whilst being one of the conspirators. Brutus seems to see himself as high-minded, moral, honourable and dignified but you will have to decide how far you think this is really true of him.

Friendship

The argument degenerates into a childish squabble. Cassius offers Brutus his dagger and says he should stab him in the heart if he dislikes him so much. Brutus replies that he will do nothing of the sort. He was angry but now he is calm again. Both men admit to being ill-tempered. A poet forces his way in, concerned that the two men should not be left alone if they are arguing. Cassius is tolerant of the poet's outburst but Brutus commands him to get out.

'O Cassius, I am sick of many griefs'

Portia

Brutus reveals that his short temper is in part explained by the news of Portia's suicide. She was afraid that the great army of Antony and Octavius would destroy Brutus and she took her own life by swallowing coals. Fire is a recurring image in the play and often appears in connection with images of death and hell as a punishment or warning from heaven, as in the storm before Caesar's murder.

The two men drink a toast to their mended friendship. Messengers report that the army of Antony and Octavius is approaching the town of Philippi and that many senators have been put to death. Messala, one of the messengers, reveals that he has had a letter telling of Portia's death. He is amazed at how calmly Brutus takes this news, unconscious that Brutus already knew.

Some commentators think that Shakespeare meant to take out one of the two passages where **Brutus** talks about **Portia's death**, but that somehow they were both left in. When Brutus talks to Cassius he reacts as an ordinary man who is upset by bad news. This increases the audience's sympathy for him. When Messala reveals the bad news Brutus is either cold and inhuman, or is putting on an act in front of his servants, depending on your point of view.

Brutus changes the subject and asks what the others think of marching their own army towards Philippi. Typically, although Brutus asks Cassius for his opinion it is clear that he has already made up his mind and ignores Cassius when he tries to butt in. Cassius seems to give up trying to influence Brutus. Perhaps he feels sorry about Brutus' wife and is glad that they have made friends again; it is hard to know. Brutus may be in charge but his inexperience shows here and he makes his final mistake when he decides that they will march to Philippi, against the sensible tactical advice of Cassius. Brutus argues that they must act now because their army is at the height of its power. He says: 'There is a tide in the affairs of men,/Which, taken at the flood, leads on to fortune…'

Order, disorder and power

Ironically, he says that their power cannot get stronger so it must grow weaker if they wait; the only way now is downwards, but he fails to see that this is about to come true. Maybe Brutus is driven by a feeling that his time has come and that he really has no choice unless he wants to spend his life in misery.

After the others have gone, Brutus asks Lucius to play him some music. Lucius falls asleep and Brutus begins to read. In private Brutus reverts to the civilised man you saw with Portia.

'Thy evil spirit, Brutus'

Caesar's ghost appears and gives Brutus the ominous message that it will meet him again at Philippi. After his brief moment of peace this vision has come to torment Brutus. Notice that the ghost describes itself as Brutus' evil spirit – meaning perhaps that it is a spirit which will be bad for Brutus, but perhaps also that it is a product of the evil murderer that is Brutus. Brutus said in Act 2 Sc 1 that he wanted to destroy Caesar's spirit, but that is the one thing that he has not been able to do.

Harmony has gone from the world

Order, disorder and power

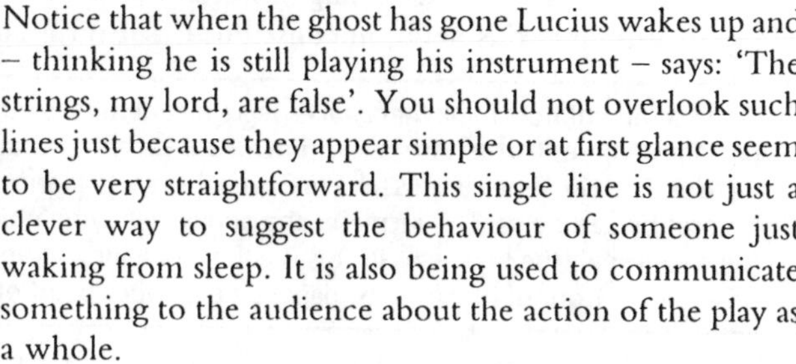

Notice that when the ghost has gone Lucius wakes up and – thinking he is still playing his instrument – says: 'The strings, my lord, are false'. You should not overlook such lines just because they appear simple or at first glance seem to be very straightforward. This single line is not just a clever way to suggest the behaviour of someone just waking from sleep. It is also being used to communicate something to the audience about the action of the play as a whole.

Fate and the supernatural

Lucius says that his instrument is out of tune, but the audience in Shakespeare's day would understand this as a reference to the lack of harmony that would now exist in the world at large as well. Perhaps because of the actions of the conspirators, the world has fallen into chaos – into a state where things are no longer in harmony with each other. Caesar has been brutally murdered, dreadful storms and visions have appeared, friends have become enemies, families have turned against each other, Portia has taken her own life, armies are massing to destroy each other and ghosts have begun to walk the earth.

Antony begins to gather his power in his single-minded search for revenge. He is shown as a man without conscience in the way he pursues his mission. Nothing is allowed to stand in his way and he is prepared to sacrifice even his own relatives. He is an example of how morally destructive vengeance can be to a peaceful, ordered life.

Disorder and chaos are also starting to appear amongst the conspirators. Their firm purpose begins to break down as they squabble like children. The disorder that they have brought into the world begins to touch them as Portia dies unnaturally, their own sense of justice is sacrificed for their own survival, and Caesar's ghost returns to earth to visit Brutus.

Many of the people of Shakespeare's time believed that the world was governed by forces beyond human control. These forces – sometimes collected together and given the name of fate – could not be understood by human beings. The **ghost of Caesar** is an example of these forces. The ghost may also represent Brutus' guilt and his own doubts about the murder. Brutus is a man who may be starting to realise that what he has done is evil and that his past deeds are about to catch up with him.

Self-test (Questions) Act Four

Uncover the plot

Antony, Octavius and Lepidus meet to decide who they shall blame/imprison/kill as traitors to Caesar. At the camp near Stresa/Sardis/Syria, Brutus fears that Cassius' friendship is cooling and, when he arrives, Cassius accuses Brutus of deceiving/delaying/wronging him. In private, Brutus accuses Cassius of withholding arms/money/food from him and Cassius replies that he is a more experienced soldier than Brutus. Brutus tells Cassius of Calphurnia's/Portia's/Flavia's suicide, and Cassius defers to Brutus' judgement that their armies should march to Rome/Philippi/Syracuse and fight Antony and Octavius there. That night, Ciciero's/Caesar's/Portia's ghost appears to Brutus, saying that it will see him again at Philippi.

Who? Why? How? Where? What?

1 Who have their names 'pricked down' by Antony on his dealth list?
2 Who is a 'slight unmeritable man, meet to be sent on errands'?
3 Why is Cassius angry with Brutus?
4 Why is Brutus angry with Cassius?
5 How many senators have Octavius and Antony put to death?
6 Where does Brutus say their army will meet with Antony and Octavius' army?
7 What is Brutus doing when Caesar's ghost appears?
8 What does Brutus ask Caesar's ghost, and how does it reply?
9 How did Portia die?
10 What does Caesar's ghost say is the reason for its appearance?

Who said that?

1 Who said: 'There are no tricks in plain and simple faith'
2 Who said: 'I am a soldier, I/Older in practice, abler than yourself/To make condition'
3 Who said: 'O Cassius, I am sick of many griefs'
4 Who said: 'A friend should bear his friend's infirmities'
5 Who said: 'The strings, my lord, are false'

Open quotes

1 'He shall but bear them...'
2 'There is no terror, Cassius, in your threats...'
3 'There is a tide in the affairs of men...'
4 'And we must take the current when it serves...'
5 'Good reasons must of force...'

Friend or foe?

1 In time of civil war, loyalties are divided and it is important to know who can be trusted. Find THREE quotes from this Act which illustrate that a show of fiendship can sometimes be just that – a show.
2 Name three characters who have been betrayed in the play.
3 This Act contains two councils of war. Which pair of leaders do you consider the more politically aware? Why?
4 How does Shakespeare make it clear that Brutus and Cassius' arguments are public knowledge?

Ready for death

1 Brutus' reaction to Portia's death shows that he has thought about death and accepted its inevitability. Find another occasion in the play when Brutus expresses this philosophy.
2 Who else in the play has a similar attitude?
3 Find two occasions on which Brutus has said he would rather be dead than live in dishonour.

Self-test (Answers) Act Four

Uncover the plot

Antony, Octavius and Lepidus meet to decide who they shall kill as traitors to Caesar. At the camp near Sardis, Brutus fears that Cassius' friendship is cooling and, when he arrives, Cassius accuses Brutus of wronging him. In private, Brutus accuses Cassius of withholding money for Brutus' arms and Cassius replies that he is a more experienced soldier than Brutus. Brutus then tells Cassius of Portia's suicide, and Cassius defers to Brutus' judgement that their armies should march to Philippi and fight Antony and Octavius there. That night, Caesar's ghost appears to Brutus, saying that it will see him again at Philippi.

Who? What? Why? How?

1 Lepidus' brother and Antony's nephew (his sister's son) Publius
2 Lepidus
3 Because Brutus has punished one of Cassius's soldiers for taking bribes
4 Because Cassius has refused to send money to pay the army
5 One hundred
6 On the plains at Philippi
7 Brutus is reading a book
8 'Art thou any thing?' 'Thy evil spirit, Brutus'
9 She swallowed coals of fire
10 To tell Brutus that is will see him at Philippi

Who said that?

1 Brutus 4,2
2 Cassius 4,3
3 Brutus 4,3
4 Cassius 4,3
5 Lucius 4,3

Open quotes

1 'He shall but bear them as the ass bears gold' Antony 4,1
2 'There is no terror, Cassius, in your threats,/For I am armed so strong in honesty/That they pass by me as the idle wind' Brutus 4,3
3 'There is a tide in the affairs of men,/Which, taken at the flood, leads on to fortune' Brutus 4,3
4 'And we must take the current when it serves/Or lose our ventures' Brutus 4,3
5 'Good reasons must of force give place to better' Brutus 4,3

Friend or foe?

1 1 '...some that smile have in their hearts, I fear,/Millions of mischiefs' Antony 4,1
2 '...hollow men, like horses hot at hand,/Make gallant show and promise of their mettle' Brutus 4,1
3 'The people 'twixt Philippi and this ground/Do stand but in a forced affection' Brutus 4,3
2 Caesar when he was stabbed 3,1; Brutus in allowing Antony to speak 3,2; Lepidus when Antony and Octavius dismiss him behind his back 4,1
3 Antony and Octavius. The relationship between them is less personal and they do not waste time in private disputes
4 He introduces a poet who has written a verse on the subject

Ready for death

1 Brutus: 'That we shall die, we know; 'tis but the time/And drawing days out, that men stand upon' 3,1
2 Caesar: 'Cowards die many times before their death/The valiant never taste of death but once' 2,2;
Cassius: 'Why, he that cuts off twenty years of life/Cuts off so many years of fearing death' 3,1
3 'I love the name of honour more than I fear death' 1,3; 'I have the same dagger for myself, when it shall please my country to need my death' 3,2;

Act 5 Scene 1

The army of Antony and Octavius meets the army of Brutus and Cassius. The two sides' leaders meet and exchange insults. Brutus and Cassius say farewell to each other before the battle in case they do not meet again.

Octavius is pleased that the army of Brutus and Cassius has arrived on the plains at Philippi. Cassius' judgement is shown to have been sound. Octavius reminds Antony that it was he who thought the enemy would keep to the hills, which would make it difficult for them to be attacked, and that he was wrong. Antony remarks that the enemy are pretending to be confident by coming down to meet them, but that he knows they are not.

As if to contradict Antony, the opposing army advances in full battle array, ready to begin the fight. Notice how the squabble between Brutus and Cassius in the previous Act is mirrored here. Antony and Octavius quarrel about who will have which side of the field to attack. Brutus and Cassius appear and Antony and Octavius begin the traditional pre-battle exchange of words with them.

Antony reminds Brutus of the way the conspirators bowed before Caesar and kissed his feet, whilst Casca was creeping up to stab him from behind. Cassius points out that if it had been left to him Antony would have died with Caesar. Octavius draws his sword and says he will not sheathe it until every one of Caesar's thirty-three wounds are avenged. Cassius calls Octavius a 'peevish schoolboy' and Antony a 'masquer and a reveller' (someone who spends all his time at parties and in drinking). Brutus and Cassius seem to come out of these exchanges as second best.

Cassius worries about bad omens

Fate and the supernatural

Cassius confides to Messala, one of his followers, that he is worried. He feels that he is being forced to risk everything on the outcome of this one battle. He once sneered at Caesar's superstitious behaviour, but now he thinks differently. He says that when they were travelling from Sardis, two eagles accompanied them and let the soldiers feed them meat. This seemed like a good omen, suggesting that their army would be victorious. But now that they have arrived at Philippi, the eagles have been replaced by ravens, crows and kites that circle overhead. These seem to Cassius to be bad omens. Both Cassius and Brutus seem to feel that things are going against them. Their behaviour and speeches during this scene are very negative, in contrast to the confidence of Antony and Octavius.

'For ever, and for ever, farewell...'

Cassius tells Brutus that although he is confident they will succeed, the future is always uncertain and he wonders what Brutus will do if they lose this battle. Both men have been brooding on their own deaths. Brutus says he will not wait to be paraded through the streets of Rome, if he is defeated. The suggestion is that they will both commit suicide rather than be captured or defeated. In case they do not meet again, they decide to say farewell to each other. There is a feeling that these are genuine friends whose 'parting was well made'. This is, in fact, the last time they will see each other alive.

> **Cassius and Brutus** behave here in public more in the way they have up to now behaved in private. **Cassius** wants them both to survive the battle, not for any riches or lofty rewards, but only so that they may grow old as friends together. But he seems resigned to defeat and death. **Brutus** also abandons his unemotional attitude. At their parting they are simply two good friends saying farewell.

Act 5 Scene 2

This very short scene shows a corner of the battlefield. Brutus sends a messenger with urgent instructions for the other legions to attack at once, as he has seen 'cold demeanour' (a lack of fighting spirit) in Octavius' soldiers.

Act 5 Scene 3

Brutus' lack of military judgement is exposed. He moved too early and his men have started to loot the bodies of Octavius' men, assuming that the battle is won. But Cassius is surrounded by Antony's soldiers and some of his men have started to run away. Pindarus tells Cassius to flee for his life as the soldiers of Antony set fire to Cassius' camp tents. You now learn that Cassius – the man who once sneered at Caesar for his lack of physical perfection – is short-sighted. He cannot see if far-off troops are friends or enemies and he sends Titinius to see whether the troops are friend or foe.

Cassius' defective eyesight is symbolic of his lack of perception in other ways. He has been short-sighted in thinking that the conspiracy to kill Caesar would achieve anything but chaos by itself. He has not had the foresight to realise the unwisdom of destroying Caesar because of what he *might* become.

'My life is run his compass'

Today is Cassius' birthday – another bad omen he thinks – and he says that

Fate and the supernatural

time has come round again to its starting point for him and that his life has run to its end. This is another example of Cassius's short-sightedness; he cannot see any further than the immediate present. Because things are not all good, Cassius assumes that they must be all bad – this is the same mistake he made about Caesar.

'Caesar, thou art revenged, even with the sword that killed thee'

Pindarus sees Cassius' best friend Titinius surrounded by horsemen and thinks he has been captured. Cassius says he is ashamed to have lived so long to see his friend captured in front of him. Feeling a coward, Cassius gives Pindarus his sword and commands that he kill him. As he dies, Cassius says that Caesar is revenged because this is the same sword that Cassius murdered him with.

Order, disorder and power

Titinius arrives. He was not captured by horsemen after all. They were Brutus' men come to tell of the defeat of Octavius and to give a victory wreath to Cassius. Titinius is saddened by the death of Cassius: the 'sun of Rome is set'. The imagery of fire returns again in the red rays of the setting sun and the red blood that means that 'Cassius' day is set'. Titinius sends Messala to give the bad news to Brutus, then takes his own life because he blames himself for Cassius' death.

'O Julius Caesar, thou art mighty yet!'

Brutus enters and sees the bodies of Cassius and Titinius. He says that the spirit of Caesar lives on to 'turn our swords in our own proper entrails'. Leaving his dead friends, Brutus returns to the battle against Antony, vowing to find time later to honour Cassius properly and saying that he will weep then.

Act 5 Scene 4

Friendship

Lucilius pretends to be Brutus and dares the enemy to fight him. Antony's soldiers know that Brutus would be a valuable prize, so refuse to kill him. Antony recognises that Lucilius is not Brutus and commands that he be well cared for. Echoing his earlier remarks to the conspirators, he says that he would rather have such men as his friends than enemies. Antony seems to have changed from the man who made lists of those to die. Perhaps he feels that more killing will accomplish nothing, or perhaps he simply respects courage and loyalty.

Act 5 Scene 5

In a corner of the battlefield, Brutus asks two of his remaining followers – Clitus and Dardanius – to kill him, but they refuse. He sits and weeps at the way events have gone. He tells another of his followers, Volumnius, about Caesar's ghost and says that it has visited him again here at Philippi. Brutus fees that his hour is come. It is touching that in order to try to persuade Volumnius to help him die with dignity he reminds him that they went to school together. Volumnius refuses, because he considers himself Brutus' friend.

Friendship

Like Caesar and Cassius before him, Brutus at the end values loyalty and friendship above everything else. This is sad because there have been several times when men have not been honest with him: his friend Cassius, for one. Brutus still does not see the political world as it really is, but as he would like it to be.

As the enemy closes in, Brutus tells his men to flee. Clitus, who has been asleep through Brutus's efforts to persuade the others to help him die, remains. He agrees to hold Brutus' sword whilst he runs onto it.

Brutus is more content at taking his own life than he was in taking the life of Caesar. He was never really comfortable with taking part in Caesar's murder and throughout the play there has been a conflict between Brutus the 'honourable' public man and Brutus the private 'emotional' man.

'This was the noblest Roman of them all'

Antony and Octavius learn of Brutus' death. Antony says that of all the conspirators, only Brutus genuinely believed he acted for the best. All the other conspirators acted out of envy. This makes him 'the noblest of them all'.

Antony acknowledges the 'private' side of Brutus by recounting how he was essentially a gentle person: 'His life was gentle...'. This may be the side of Brutus that Antony saw, but you have seen a different side of Brutus – a man plagued by doubts and continually misled by an unrealistic, idealistic view of the world.

Cassius and Brutus begin to see reality creeping up on them. Cassius becomes alarmed at the bad omens surrounding them. Brutus reveals that he could not cope with the shame of defeat. Both men have chanced their lives on this one battle.

Events go badly wrong. Both men show poor judgement that leads to their deaths. Both men die realising that friendship and loyalty are more valuable than the things they have been fighting for.

Cassius dies because of his own impetuosity. He is an opportunist who rushes too quickly into things without thinking them through.

Only at the very end of his life do you get a glimpse that **Brutus** might have realised his terrible mistake in murdering Caesar. Brutus was a man who thought that the politics of logic could somehow produce a world in which evil was impossible. This turned out to be his biggest but not his only mistake.

Self-test (Questions) Act Five

Uncover the plot

Delete two of the three alternatives given, to find the correct plot. Beware possible misconceptions and muddles.

The two armies meet on the plains/hills/marshes of Philippi. When the leaders meet, they exchange greetings/tokens of friendship/insults. Then, before battle commences, Brutus and Cassius say hail!/farewell/oaths to each other. This is the last time they will meet for a year/again/for six months. On the battlefield, Brutus'/Cassius'/Octavius' tactics are flawed: he sends his army to attack the enemy because he judges them to be cowardly/tired/weak. Thinking the battle lost, Pindarus helps Cassius to die by stabbing him. Lepidus/Lucilius/Lucius pretends to be Brutus, but Antony recognises him and takes him prisoner. The battle lost, Brutus requests his servant Clitus/Cassius/Cicero and Dardanius to kill him to spare him the dishonour /inconvenience/annoyance of being taken prisoner. They refuse, but Servius/Strato/Sennus, another servant, holds up Brutus' sword whilst Brutus runs upon it. Antony delivers Brutus' epitaph: 'This was the noblest Roman/truest soldier/bravest man of them all.'

Why? How? What? Who?

1 Why does Antony think the army of Brutus and Cassius has come to meet them on the plain?
2 Why do Antony and Octavius disagree about battle tactics?
3 How many wounds does Octavius say Caesar had?
4 What is special about the day of the battle for Cassius?
5 What omens have worried Cassius?
6 What does Brutus say he will not do if they lose the battle?
7 Who set Cassius' camp tents on fire?
8 Who pretends to be Brutus?
9 Who went to school with Brutus?
10 How will Octavius and Antony make peace with the enemy army?

Who said that?

1 Who said: 'Good words are better than bad strokes'
2 Who said: 'Defiance, traitors, hurl we in your teeth.'
3 Who said: 'For ever and for ever, farewell.'
4 Who said: 'The sun of Rome is set! Our day is gone.'
5 Who said: 'I had rather have/Such men for my friends than enemies'

Open quotes

Find the line – and complete the phrase or sentence.

1 'A peevish schoolboy...'
2 'Why now blow wind, swell billow and swim bark!...'
3 'My heart doth joy that yet in all my life...'
4 'Caesar, now be still...'
5 'His life was gentle, and the elements/So mix'd in him...'

Eyeball to eyeball

The exchange of insults between the opposing generals is full of echoes. Where else in the play have you heard similar phrases to these?

1 'You show'd your teeth like apes and fawn'd like hounds' 5,1
2 'You have stol'n their buzzing, Antony/And very wisely threat before you sting' 5,1
3 'Oh, you flatterers!' 5,1
4 'bow'd like bondmen, kissing Caesar's feet/Whilst damned Casca, like a cur...'5,1
5 'Joined with a masker and a reveller' 5,1
6 'Never, till Caesar's three and thirty wounds/Be well avenged' 5,2

What makes you think so?

1 Find FOUR quotations which make you think that Brutus and Cassius know they are to die that day.
2 Brutus considers suicide (5,1). Who else in the play does this call to mind?

Self-test (Answers) Act Five

Uncover the plot

The two armies meet on the plains of Philippi. When the leaders meet, they exchange insults. Then, before battle commences, Brutus and Cassius say farewell to each other. This is the last time they will meet again. On the battlefield, Brutus' tactics are flawed: he sends his army to attack the enemy because he judges them to be weak. Thinking the battle lost, Pindarus helps Cassius to die by stabbing him. Lucilius pretends to be Brutus, but Antony recognises him and takes him prisoner. The battle lost, Brutus requests his servant Clitus and Dardanius to kill him to spare him the dishonour of being taken prisoner. They refuse, but Strato, another servant, holds up Brutus' sword whilst Brutus runs upon it. Antony delivers Brutus' epitaph: 'This was the noblest Roman of them all.'

Why? How? What? Who?

1 To convice the enemy that they feel confident and courageous
2 They both wish to lead the attack on the left-hand side of the plain
3 Thirty-three
4 It is his birthday
5 Two eagles which have followed the army from Sardis have been replaced by 'ravens, crows and kites'
6 Be taken back to Rome as a prisoner
7 Antony's soldiers
8 Lucilius
9 Volumnius
10 They will not recriminate against them, but will accept them as their followers

Who said that?

1 Brutus 5,1
2 Octavius 5,1
3 Brutus and Cassius to each other 5,1
4 Titinius 5,3
5 Antony 5,4

Open quotes

1 'A peevish schoolboy, worthless of such honour' Cassius 5,1
2 'Why now blow wind, swell billow and swim bark!/The storm is up, and all is on the hazard' Cassius 5,1
3 'My heart doth joy that yet in all my life/I found no man but he was true to me' Brutus 5,5
4 'Caesar, now be still,/I kill'd not thee with half so good a will' Brutus 5,5
5 'His life was gentle, and the elements/So mix'd in him that Nature might stand up/And say to all the world "This was a man!"' Antony 5,5

Eyeball to eyeball

1 'I spurn thee like a cur out of my way' Caesar 3,1
2 'And then I grant, we put a sting in him' Brutus 2,1
3 'I kiss thy hand, but not in flattery' Brutus 3,1
'but when I tell him he hates flatterers/He says he does, being then most flattered' Decius 2,1
4 'Sweet words/Low crooked court'sies and base spaniel fawning' Caesar 3,1
5 'for he is given/To sports, to wildness and much company' Brutus 2,1
6 'Over thy wounds do I now prophesy…Domestic fury and fierce civil strife…That this foul deed shall smell above the earth' Antony 3,1

What makes you think so?

1 'For ever and for ever, farewell!' 5,1
'As we were sickly prey' 5,1
'Their shadows seem/A canopy most fatal' 5,1
'This day I breathed my first: time is come round' 5,3
2 Portia, who committed suicide – and who reminded Brutus that she was Cato's daughter (who also, famously, killed himself) 2,2

Quotations you should know

Why, man, he doth bestride the narrow world
Like a Colossus, and we petty men
Walk under his huge legs, and peep about
To find ourselves dishonourable graves.

(Cassius) Act 1 Sc 2

Cowards die many times before their deaths;
The valiant never taste of death but once.
Of all the wonders that I yet have heard,
It seems to me most strange that men should fear,
Seeing that death, a necessary end,
Will come when it will come.

Act 2 Sc 2

...I am constant as the northern star,
Of whose true fixed and resting quality
There is no fellow in the firmament.

Act 3 Sc 1

Set honour in one eye, and death i' th' other,
And I will look on both indifferently:

Act 1 Sc 2

Let us be sacrificers, but not butchers, Caius.

Act 2 Sc 1

...not that I loved Caesar less, but that I loved Rome more.

Act 3 Sc 2

There is a tide in the affairs of men,
Which, taken at the flood, leads on to fortune;
Omitted, all the voyage of their life
Is bound in shallows and in miseries.

Act 4 Sc 3

This was the noblest Roman of them all.
All the conspirators save only he
Did that they did in envy of great Caesar;
He only, in a general honest thought
And common good to all, made one of them.
His life was gentle, and the elements
So mixed in him, that Nature might stand up
And say to all the world, 'This was a man!'

(Antony) Act 5 Sc 5

Yond Cassius has a lean and hungry look;
He thinks too much: such men are dangerous.

(Caesar) Act 1 Sc 2

Cassius from bondage will deliver Cassius.
Therein, ye gods, you make the weak most strong;
Therein, ye gods, you tyrants do defeat.

Act 1 Sc 3

...Caesar's spirit, ranging for revenge,
With Ate by his side, come hot from hell,
Shall in these confines, with a monarch's voice
Cry, 'Havoc!' and let slip the dogs of war,

Act 3 Sc 1

Friends, Romans, countrymen, lend me your ears;
I come to bury Caesar, not to praise him.
The evil that men do lives after them,
The good is oft interrèd with their bones;
So let it be with Caesar. The noble Brutus
Hath told you Caesar was ambitious.
If it were so, it was a grievous fault,
And grievously hath Caesar answered it.
Here, under leave of Brutus and the rest–
For Brutus is an honourable man;
So are they all, all honourable men–
Come I to speak in Caesar's funeral.
...
I come not, friends, to steal away your hearts;
I am no orator, as Brutus is,
But, as you know me all, a plain blunt man,
That love my friend;

Act 3 Sc 2